JUST HIERARCHY

Just Hierarchy

WHY SOCIAL HIERARCHIES MATTER IN CHINA AND THE REST OF THE WORLD

DANIEL A. BELL

WANG PEI

PRINCETON UNIVERSITY PRESS

PRINCETON & OXFORD

Copyright © 2020 by Princeton University Press

Requests for permission to reproduce material from this work
should be sent to permissions@press.princeton.edu

Published by Princeton University Press
41 William Street, Princeton, New Jersey 08540
6 Oxford Street, Woodstock, Oxfordshire OX20 1TR

press.princeton.edu

All Rights Reserved

Library of Congress Control Number 2019954572
ISBN 978-0-691-20089-7
ISBN (e-book) 978-0-691-20088-0

British Library Cataloging-in-Publication Data is available

Editorial: Rob Tempio and Matt Rohal
Production Editorial: Jill Harris
Jacket Design: Carmina Alvarez
Production: Brigid Ackerman
Publicity: Alyssa Sanford and Kate Farquhar-Thomson
Copyeditor: Jay Boggis

This book has been composed in Arno Pro

Printed on acid-free paper. ∞

Printed in the United States of America

10 9 8 7 6 5 4 3 2 1

CONTENTS

v

ACKNOWLEDGMENTS

FIRST BUT NOT LEAST, we would like to thank each other. The ideas in this book evolved via prolonged conversations and arguments over the past few years, to the point that we forgot who said what. Daniel wrote most of the English version of this book, and Pei wrote most of the Chinese version, but we are jointly responsible for its ideas, whether good or bad. We are most grateful to Rob Tempio, our insightful and supportive editor at Princeton University Press, along with two anonymous referees who allowed us to further refine our ideas. We are also grateful to our research assistant, Sun Qiming, and Daniel would like to thank his assistants at Shandong University—Liu Yuhan, Huang Ping, Wang Fuxiang, and Wang Chengchao—for help. We would also like to thank Cheng Jiaolong for writing the beautiful calligraphy on the book's back cover.

Daniel owes special thanks to family members for emotional and intellectual support. He would also like to thank Kong Lingdong, Cao Xianqiang, Kong Xinfeng, Liu Lin, and all his other colleagues and leaders at Shandong University's School of Political Science and Public Administration for providing an intellectually stimulating setting that allowed him to write this book. Daniel is also grateful to Tsinghua University president Qiu Yong for continued support at Tsinghua as well as his coteacher at Schwarzman College, Wang Hui, for fascinating discussions on Chinese intellectual history, Bai Tongdong at Fudan

University for inspiring conversations in political theory, and Eric X. Li for friendship that goes beyond the ordinary meaning of friendship. He would also like to thank his students at Shandong University and Tsinghua University for constructive and often well-deserved criticism of the teacher's ideas.

Daniel also owes special thanks to Nicolas Berggruen. We cannot construct a better world without serious engagement with the world's ideas—including ideas from previously marginalized parts of the world—and Nicolas has both the vision and the means to realize this aspiration. The idea for this book emerged when Daniel was director of the Berggruen Institute's Center for Philosophy and Culture. Daniel helped to organize a conference on "Hierarchy and Equality" at Stanford University's Center for the Advanced Study in the Behavioral Sciences in March 2016. The papers were excellent—and we have made use of several of them in this book—and Daniel realized that there's the need for a full-length book on the topic of "Just Hierarchy." Daniel would like to thank the workshop's participants as well as co-organizers Margaret Conley and Jennifer Bourne for help and inspiration. He would also like to thank Berggruen Institute leadership in Los Angeles: Nathan Gardels, Dawn Nakagawa, Nils Gilman, and (former) president Craig Calhoun for help over the years. Daniel owes special thanks to the Berggruen Institute's China Center at Peking University which supported several workshops in New Delhi, Qingdao, Beijing, and Bangkok, comparing Chinese and Indian thought, and Daniel is grateful to workshop participants as well as to co-organizers Song Bing, Roger Ames, Yan Xuetong, Amitav Acharya, Rajeev Bhargava, Shelley Hu, Li Xiaojiao, and Li He.

Pei would like to thank her friends and colleagues at Fudan University's China Institute. She is particularly grateful to Zhang Weiwei, Eric X. Li, Fan Yongpeng, Chen Ping, Li Bo, Yu Liang,

Lin Ling, Meng Weizhan, and Feng Zhun. She would also like to thank visitors to the China Institute, especially Alexander Dugin, Yukon Huang, Martin Jacques, Kishore Mahbubani, and Dominique de Villepin. She is grateful to the institute for providing time and support and an intellectually stimulating environment for research.

Pei owes much to Wang Hui for constant concern and intellectual inspiration. Wang Hui supervised Pei's postdoctoral research at Tsinghua University and showed the importance of relating philosophy to real politics and social life. Pei would also like to thank her former colleagues at the Tsinghua Institute for Advanced Study in the Humanities and Social Sciences (TIAS): Kong Yuan, Fu Zheng, Yuan Xianxin, Li Peiyan, and Yang Tao, as well as visitors to TIAS, Michael Dutton, Viren Murthy, and Yu Zhizhong. Pei and Daniel are also grateful to Geir Helgesen, Liu Chunrong, and Unn Irene Aasdalen for facilitating and modeling the best form of cross-cultural dialogue at Nansen Academy in Lillehammer, Norway.

Pei's friends Cheng Jiaolong, Li Shuzhi, and Wang Hairong have provided unconditional support and have inspired her with new perspectives on reality. Pei is deeply indebted to her family members and especially to her mother, who always surprises with her direct and sharp comments, and spoils Pei with all her tenderness.

Earlier versions of chapter 2 were published in *Philosophy and Public Issues* (by Pei) and the *Journal of Chinese Humanities /* 文史哲 (by Daniel), and we are grateful to the publications for permission to draw on those articles, as well as to *Aeon* for permission to publish the online appendix. Earlier versions of chapter 2 were presented (by Daniel and Pei) at the University of Malaya's Institute of China Studies, the Penang Institute, the Beijing Thinkers' Forum, and the annual Reset conference in

Venice; and (by Daniel) as a keynote speech at the 2019 IPP International Conference on Civilization and National Governance in Guangzhou, at the Political Meritocracy in Comparative Historical Perspective conference and the China India Meritocracy conference, both at the Harvard Center in Shanghai, and at the Nansen Academy in Lillehammer, Norway. Earlier versions of chapter 3 were presented (by Daniel) at "From a Westcentric to Post-Westcentric World" in Taipei, at the Peking University's Berggruen China Center, and at CKGSB in Beijing. Earlier versions of chapter 5 were presented (by Daniel and Pei) at Santa Clara University and (by Daniel) at Pembroke College, Cambridge University (as the annual China Goes Global lecture), at Sun Yat-Sen University (as a Global Justice Lecture), at Xi'an Jiaotong–Liverpool University (as a keynote speech at the Second Annual Conference of the Jiangnan Research Group on China Studies), at Peking University's Berggruen China Center, and at the Nansen Academy in Lillehammer, Norway. Formal settings that allow us to refine our arguments are important, but informal settings that allow for the expression of half-baked ideas even more so. We are grateful to friends who share our love of crazy conversation fueled by fine wine and good food.

JUST HIERARCHY

Introduction

THE SEATING ARRANGEMENTS for formal meals in Shandong province—the home of Confucian culture, with a population of nearly 100 million people—are rigidly hierarchical. The host with the highest social status sits at the "top" of a round table with a view of the door, the host with the second-highest social status sits at the other end of the table; the guest with the highest social status sits on the right-hand side of the host with the highest social status and next to the host with the third-highest social status; the guest with the second-highest social status sits on left side of the host with the highest social status and next to the host with the fourth-highest social status; the guest with the third-highest social status sits on the right side of the host with the second-highest social status and next to host with the fifth-highest social status; the guest with the fourth-highest social status sits on the left side of the host with the second-highest social status and next to the host with the sixth-highest social status. The other seats are randomly distributed among those with the least social status, with the number of randomly assigned seats depending on the number of hosts and guests. Sounds complex? The pictorial depiction of the social hierarchy in figure 1 might be helpful.[1]

What's wrong with Shandong's seating arrangements for formal meals? Nothing at all! The only thing wrong is the expectation that all social relations are supposed to be equal. As dean

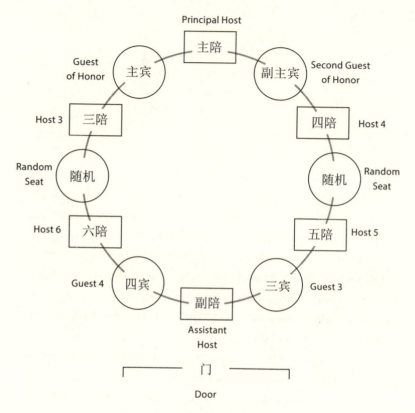

FIGURE 1. Seating hierarchy for dinner party.

at Shandong University's school of political science and public administration, Daniel has hosted countless meals with such seating arrangements, including hosting of foreign guests, and he has not once received any complaints. Perhaps his guests are too polite to complain. But we'd like to think that such seating arrangements are tolerated because they do not express and reinforce unjust hierarchies that rank people according to race or gender. People who are not ethnically Chinese—such as Daniel—are seated in the same position as ethnically Chinese people with the same social status (i.e., with a title of dean). Men and women occupy their seats according to their social roles regardless of gender: For example, President Fan of Shandong University is female, and she occupies the principal host seat at formal meals, in the same position as previous (male) presidents at Shandong University. This is not to deny that patriarchal ways still inform the seating arrangements in rural parts of Shandong province—women often sit at different and less comfortable tables—but such norms are rejected in university settings.[2] The seating arrangements at Shandong University are also tolerated because the hierarchies are nearly invisible to the untrained eye. The tables are round, with the appearance of perfectly equal symmetry,[3] and the visiting guests won't know about the social hierarchies unless they are informed of the norms by local hosts. In contrast, the rectangular "high tables" at traditional Oxford and Cambridge universities are literally higher than tables for students, and students are not allowed to start eating until the teachers formally get the proceedings under way. Whatever the case for special treatment (better food and wine) for teachers and guests in university settings, Oxbridge-style "in your face" social hierarchies often generate a vague sense of unease even for beneficiaries of these arrangements.

But we'd like to defend a stronger claim. It's not just a matter of tolerating Shandong-style seating arrangements because they do not express unjust or visible hierarchies. These arrangements are endorsed, and even enjoyed, because they express several of the virtues of what we call "just hierarchies," that is, morally justified rankings of people or groups with respect to valued social dimensions. Consider the distribution of seats for persons of higher social status in Shandong. The usual "fight" among those in the know is to refuse a seat with more social prestige. So there is a toss and struggle, and finally the "loser" of the battle will give in and reluctantly take the seat that expresses a higher social position. Most often, both sides know the outcome of the struggle—for example, the dean will take the seat of the principal host if he or she has the highest rank in the university hierarchy, the guest with the most academic prestige and/or the greatest number of years of physical existence (i.e., the oldest person) will take the seat of the guest of honor, and so on—but it would seem immodest to immediately claim one's "rightful" position (the foreigners who are ignorant of such rituals often take their assigned seats without putting up a struggle, but they are forgiven for their moral transgressions because they are not expected to know Shandong-style norms of civility). Put differently, the struggles, however hypocritical they may seem to the critical outsider, express Confucian-style virtues of humility and modesty.[4] Not only that, but the occupants of the seats with more social prestige have more responsibility. They must foot the bill: To be more precise, the assistant host must pay for the meal, but the funds come from the university (since the start of the anticorruption campaign in 2012, funds from public institutions do not cover alcohol, and often the principal host must bring the liquor at his or her own expense). The hosts are responsible for treating the guests well, and each host is supposed to take care of a particular guest corresponding to her or his hierarchical role. The hierarchical seating arrangement ensures not just that the most honored guest is treated well, but that the next three most socially important guests will also get some personal care. The hosts serve the others from communal dishes in the middle, starting with the principal host serving the most important guest on the right and then the second-most-important guest on the left, and then the assistant host does the same with the third-most-important guest on the right followed by the fourth-most-important guest on the left (foreigners might start serving themselves first, but again they are forgiven for their moral transgressions on the grounds that they may not be familiar with Shandong-style norms of civility). Then the hosts must give repeated toasts to welcome the guests, anywhere from eight times in Qufu (ground zero for Confucian culture) to three toasts in other parts of Shandong province. The assistant host must then deliver some toasts (usually fewer in number than the toasts by the principal host), then the third-most-important host delivers some toasts (fewer in number than the toasts delivered by the assistant host), then the fourth-most-important host delivers some toasts (fewer in number than the toasts delivered by the third-most-important host), and so on. These toasts often express warm feelings of greeting and affection for the visitors, but ideally they are also accompanied by literate references to Chinese history and culture, leavened with some humor. When the "official" toasting is over, the occupants of the most prestigious seating positions must go around the table and individually toast and greet each visitor. From the perspective of shy or socially reticent people, these arrangements are more beneficial to the occupants in the less prestigious seats, who can enjoy the proceedings without any responsibilities. In any case, the formalities usually break down toward the end of the evening, with semi-inebriated participants roaming around the table almost at random, either joking or exchanging serious information that could not be shared with the whole group. Last but not least, the social hierarchies can shift on different occasions. If the same people (or a similar group) meet on different occasions, the roles may shift, with the guests playing the role of hosts, and vice versa, regardless of who has the most social status in society at large. And what counts as social status is not itself rigid: Sometimes it's age, sometimes it's government rank, sometimes it's academic achievement, sometimes it's perceived level of virtue, and so on.

In this sense, the social hierarchies are not fixed and can shift depending on the context. If the visiting professor is the guest, then he or she may occupy the guest of honor seating position, even if he or she does not have the highest social status outside of the university context. So yes, Shandong-style seating and drinking rituals are hierarchical, but what's wrong if they provide hospitality for the guests and generate a sense of harmony among participants? Perhaps such hierarchies are morally justified if they shift over time and if those with more social power end up caring about the needs of those with less power and eventually do more to serve their interests? Not to mention that these hierarchical rituals are often aesthetically pleasing (the food is usually varied and delicious) and thoroughly enjoyable for the participants . . .

As an ideal, we defend hierarchical Shandong-style seating arrangements, but in practice they often have a downside. Most worrisome, there is often a fine line between semi-inebriation and total (if not fatal) inebriation.[5] Surely it's no coincidence that Shandong province has the highest per capita consumption of alcohol in mainland China (Shanghai, perhaps the most Westernized and socially egalitarian part of China, is among the lowest).[6] But there are social mechanisms that have the effect of moderating alcohol consumption: It is the highest form of rudeness to serve oneself alcohol and to drink alone in a group setting (it is similar in Confucian-influenced Korea; in the West, the first toast is often communal, but then people often serve themselves and drink without toasting others). And there is usually accommodation for those who do not drink alcohol: Their glasses are filled with water, which looks like fiery "white" alcohol (白酒), and they can join participants in group toasts without drinking alcohol. That said, we need to recognize that the social pressure to drink alcohol may not always be welcome.

Lower-ranking people often find it hard to refuse the toasts of their superiors, even if they have exceeded their "normal" levels of inebriation. Even higher-ranking people might feel unwelcome pressure to drink, as a way of showing authority over lower-ranking people or to impress guests. And guests themselves often feel unwelcome pressure to drink.[7] Chinese women who typically drink far less than men may feel somewhat alienated from the drinking rituals.[8] And sometimes the people from China's more socially egalitarian southern provinces find that Shandong-style rituals, even when they work well according to modernized social norms, are not as desirable as they might be. It may be true that universities in Shandong have shed the most egregious patriarchal norms, but there is no serious effort to honor women or recognize their special contribution to society. In Zhejiang, by contrast, the wives and children of invited guests are sometimes asked to sit in the principal guest of honor position: As a child, Pei recalls being honored as the principal guest in banquets with her parents and family friends, a practice that would be nearly inconceivable in Shandong. That said, it doesn't follow that Shandong people should shed hierarchical seating arrangements and hierarchical drinking and eating rituals. The task is to modernize the hierarchical rituals according to progressive social values while maintaining the advantages that make them so enjoyable, if not morally uplifting, for the participants.

The example of Shandong-style seating arrangements is meant to shed light on our theoretical concerns. Let's now turn directly to those concerns. Equality is clearly an important value—recognized and endorsed by social and political progressives in the modern world—and much has been written on the ideal and practice of equality as well as the need to equalize relations between ethnic groups, genders, and classes. We generally share these egalitarian outlooks and concerns. But hierarchy, arguably, is equally important, and research on hierarchy has lagged behind. All complex and large-scale societies need to be organized along certain hierarchies, but the concept of hierarchy has become almost taboo in politically progressive circles. This is a huge mistake. It is important to think about which forms of hierarchy are justified and how they can be made compatible with egalitarian goals. We need to distinguish between just and unjust forms of hierarchy and think of ways to promote the good forms and minimize the influence of bad forms. But what exactly do we mean by "hierarchy" and why does it matter today? What do we mean by "bad hierarchies" that worry people with politically progressive sensibilities? Most challenging from a theoretical perspective—and the main question we try to answer in this book—is, which forms of hierarchy are morally justified today and how can they be promoted in the future?

1. What's Wrong with Hierarchy?

In a purely descriptive sense, a hierarchy is a relation that is characterized by (a) difference and (b) ranking according to some attribute. Social hierarchies tend to have a normative dimension: They are social systems in which there is "an implicit or explicit rank of individuals or groups with respect to a valued social dimension."[9] But we need further normative justification to argue that societies *should* value those dimensions. In English, the word "hierarchy" has come to have pejorative connotations because we now think that most traditional ways of ranking people or groups are not justified from a moral point of view.

Biologists tend to speak of hierarchy in the neutral sense, and they study its origin and evolution without passing any moral judgments.[10] Hierarchy is a ubiquitous organizing principle in biology and a key reason evolution produces complex, evolvable organisms. Why did hierarchy evolve? At the level of biological neural networks, the key factor is the cost of connections: According to an influential study by computer simulation, networks without a connection cost do not evolve to be hierarchical, whereas those with a connection cost evolve to be hierarchical, and such networks exhibit higher overall performance and adapt faster to new environments.[11] Put simply, with a degree of centralization in connection-making, complex biological systems need fewer connections and things can run more efficiently. A similar mechanism seems to explain the evolution of hierarchy in larger-scale social organizations. As Peter Turchin explains, "The only way that large human groups can arrive at a common course of action is by [hierarchically] structuring interpersonal connections. . . . Societies that were larger and better organized outcompeted smaller and more shambolic ones. Hierarchical organization was one of the cultural traits that was heavily favored by the new selection regime in the Holocene [which started roughly 12,000 years ago with the end of the ice age]. . . . It's a pipe dream to imagine that a large-scale society (e.g., a million or more—a small nation by today's standards!) can be organized in a nonhierarchical, horizontal way. Hierarchy (in a neutral sense) is the only way to organize large-scale societies."[12] Just as it's impossible to efficiently connect large numbers of neural networks without hierarchy, so it's impossible to connect large numbers of people in an efficient way without a hierarchically structured social organization. In short, efficiency is a clear benefit of hierarchy.

The efficiency of hierarchy may help to explain why we like hierarchies at some unconscious level. According to one study, an abstract diagram representing hierarchy was memorized more quickly than a diagram representing equality, and the faster processing led the participants to prefer the hierarchy diagram.

And participants found it easier to make decisions about a company that was hierarchical and thus thought the hierarchical organization had more positive qualities.[13] Whatever the negative feelings about hierarchy at the conscious level, it seems that the efficiency benefits of hierarchy in our evolutionary history often prompt us to like hierarchy.[14] But efficiency *per se* is not morally justified. It depends on the ends being pursued. The Nazis built superefficient concentration camps, but they were put to use for despicable purposes. Or consider the workings of natural selection. To an important extent, we are what we are because of natural selection. The mission of natural selection is to get genes into the next generation in an efficient way, and we tend to like what's helpful for this purpose and dislike what's not. As Robert Wright puts it, "We were 'designed' by natural selection to do certain things that helped our ancestors get their genes into the next generation—things like eating, having sex, earning the esteem of other people, and outdoing rivals."[15] But we can decide that doing some of the things that made us effective gene propagators in the past are no longer desirable today. Evolution may have prompted us to value our own interests above those of others, but the costs of excessive self-regard may now outweigh the benefits. For example, natural selection designed human minds to size people up in a way that would lead to interactions that benefited the genes of the humans doing the sizing up, not to size people up accurately. Hence we tend to exaggerate the virtues of our friends and the vices of our enemies. That may be efficient for purposes of reproduction, but it also provides the psychological roots for tribalism and demonization of the "other." Upon reflection, we can decide that the social and political consequences of tribalism and warfare threaten our species, if not the whole world. If we agree that it's better to let go of things like lust and conceit and ill-will that were "programmed" into us to perpetuate our genes in an effective way, then we can promote practices such as meditation that promote compassion for all sentient beings and help to erode the psychological roots of what we now consider to be immoral behavior.[16] It may well turn out that what's efficient from the point of view of natural selection is morally wrong, and we can and should strive to challenge much of what seems "natural." In the same vein, there are good reasons to challenge many of the social hierarchies that seem natural to us. These hierarchies may have arisen for reasons of efficiency, but we need not endorse them from a moral point of view. This is not pure theory: Upon reflection, it seems obvious that many of the hierarchies from the past are morally problematic today. As historian Yuval Noah Harari puts it, "complex human societies seem to require imagined hierarchies and unjust discrimination. . . . Time and again people have created order in their societies by classifying the population into imagined categories, such as superiors, commoners, and slaves; whites and blacks; patricians and plebians; Brahmins and Shudras; or rich and poor. These categories have regulated relations between millions of humans by making some people legally, politically or socially superior to others."[17] But we have made moral progress: Today, most educated people recognize and condemn the seemingly "natural" hierarchies of our past history.[18] Most Americans, for example, now endorse statements about equality and reject statements about the value of hierarchy[19] and complain that hierarchies are inhumane, immoral, and undemocratic.[20]

Why do we now reject most traditional hierarchies? A key reason, arguably, is our unhappy experience with morally bad hierarchies in the form of racism, sexism, and caste-like distinctions between people. Few if any progressive and educated people living in modern societies defend hierarchies among classes of humans who are inherently superior or inferior based on noble birth, race, sex, or religion, although such hierarchies were commonly endorsed in the past.[21] In ancient Rome, the penalty for assault on a slave was half the penalty for assault on a free man,[22] but today slavery is (fortunately) regarded as morally obscene. Ancient Chinese thinkers argued that scholar officials should be exempt from criminal punishment,[23] but no contemporary Confucian seeks to revive such forms of inequality before the law. At some level, then, we are all egalitarians who endorse the principle of equality of basic moral and legal status for citizens. And with the possible exception of crazed terrorists, we all endorse the view that human beings, regardless of background, are equally entitled to what Michael Walzer terms "thin" human rights: rights not to be tortured, enslaved, murdered, and subject to systematic racial discrimination.[24] But we—the coauthors of this book—do more than endorse equality before the law in criminal cases and basic human rights. Our book is informed by what we might call a "progressive conservative" perspective. On the one hand, we are sympathetic to the traditional egalitarian causes of the political left, including an aversion to extremes of wealth distribution, more rights for the productive classes, more support for poor countries that unduly suffer the effects of global warming, equality between men and women, as well as equal rights for same-sex couples. In our view, many of the social hierarchies traditionally viewed as natural and just are neither natural nor just, and we can and should challenge those hierarchies: by revolutionary means, if necessary. On the other hand, we share a conservative attachment to, if not reverence for, tradition, and we recognize that some traditional hierarchies—among family members, citizens, states, humans and animals, and humans and machines—are morally defensible. We do not argue for blindly reaffirming and implementing hierarchies that may have worked in the past. But suitably reformed—so we will argue—they can be appropriate for the modern world.

2. In Defense of Hierarchy

Whatever the drawbacks of traditional forms of hierarchy, the effort to combat all forms of hierarchy is neither possible nor desirable. Complex organizations and societies need some form of hierarchy and will outcompete and outlast those that seek to abolish all forms of hierarchy. History bears out this prediction: Efforts to consciously build large-scale organizations or societies without hierarchies have failed miserably. Edmund Burke famously criticized the French revolutionaries for seeking to equalize relations of command and obedience in the military and predicted such efforts would lead to the rise of "some popular general, who understands the art of conciliating the soldiery, and who possesses the true spirit of command, [and who would] draw the eyes of men upon himself [and become] the master of the whole republic."[25] In China's Cultural Revolution, the effort to stamp out social hierarchies similarly led to mass violence and populist tyranny. In contemporary China, the populist legacies of the Cultural Revolution still poison the political atmosphere, aided by the internet that allows anonymous masses to hound social undesirables into submission. In the United States, the populist backlashes against elites empower strongmen such as Donald Trump with scant regard and respect for traditional constraints on political power. So the effort to combat all forms of hierarchy will not only fail; it may lead to something even worse from a moral point of view.

In short, the choice today is not between a society with no hierarchies and one with hierarchies, but rather between a society with unjust hierarchies that perpetuate unjust power structures and one with just hierarchies that serve morally desirable purposes. Perhaps the idea of just or morally justified hierarchies seems difficult to digest at the conscious level, especially from a modern perspective. We have suggested that Shandong-style hierarchical seating arrangements can be morally justified for formal dinner occasions, but other examples readily come to mind. We generally take hierarchies of esteem for granted: Nobody doubts that LeBron James deserves his trophy as the Most Valuable Player in the 2016 NBA playoffs by virtue of his achievements on the basketball court. And whatever the disputes about the moral worthiness of particular Nobel Peace Prize winners, few object to the principle that we can and should reward those with great moral achievements of some sort. In China, the government honors adults who are filial to their elderly parents; we can argue about the choices, but it seems hard to object to the principle of honoring those who can set a good model for others.[26] What's more controversial is the claim that morally justifiable social hierarchies should structure our social lives on an everyday basis, including our relations with loved ones. That's the claim we'd like to defend in this book.

Our target is the view that all social relations should be equal. The flip side of this view is that unequal relations are fundamentally unjust: As Jean-Jacques Rousseau lamented in his *Confessions*, "I felt, more than ever, from repeated experiences, that associations on unequal terms are always to the disadvantage of the weaker party."[27] So those who care about the interests of the weak—that is, all sensitive, progressive-minded people— should affirm the ideal of equal social relations at all times in all walks of (social) life. In the contemporary world, this ideal is often expressed in everyday (English language) speech: Think

of nine-year-olds who want to be treated as equals.[28] More sur-
prising, perhaps, the blanket defense of social equality is increasingly defended by sophisticated political theorists. In the
first few decades after the publication of John Rawls's ground-
breaking book *A Theory of Justice* (1971), Western political theorists were mainly concerned about the nature of things to be distributed equally (is it income, resources, welfare, capabilities,
or something else?) and debates about the most defensible egalitarian distributive principle (should it be pure equality, the
difference principle, sufficiency, or something else?).[29] More
recently, some theorists—let's call them "social egalitarians"—
argued that this focus on distributive principles is too narrow
and neglects the broader agendas of actual egalitarian political
movements. As Elizabeth Anderson put it, "What has happened
to the concerns of the politically oppressed? What about inequalities of race, gender, class, and caste?"[30] Nor did political
theorists obsessed with the just distribution of privately appro-
priated goods, such as income, or privately enjoyed goods, such
as welfare, pay attention to the concerns of gay and lesbian
people who seek the right to get married and the disabled who
seek access to reconfigured public spaces and campaign against
demeaning stereotypes. To remedy the problem, social egalitarians argue that equality should refer first and foremost to an
egalitarian ideal of social relations: Various goods should be distributed in order to secure a society in which people are related
as equals. The focus on social inequality allows political theorists
to critique the unjust social hierarchies that have plagued and
continue to plague human societies, "including slavery, serfdom,
debt peonage, feudalism, monarchy, oligarchy, caste and class inequality, racism, patriarchy, colonialism, and stigmatization
based on sexuality, disability, and bodily appearance."[31] So far,
so good. As political progressives, we welcome this focus on

social relations and applaud the critique of the unjust social hierarchies that have oppressed and stigmatized the large majority of people in history.[32] But it doesn't follow that equal social relations are necessarily just and that hierarchical social relations are necessarily unjust. As Joseph Chan explains, one could argue that traditional hierarchies "are problematic not because they undermine equality, but because they deprive people in the lower ranks of such hierarchies of the opportunities to pursue wellbeing and develop virtue, and they do so on ascriptive grounds that are morally irrelevant and hence unfair. Rejection of these hierarchies may not necessarily lead to endorsement of equal social relationships or rejection of other hierarchies. One could imagine hierarchies that are relatively free from the ills of these historical examples and capable of promoting the wellbeing and virtue of the lower ranked."[33] We'd like to add that not all historical hierarchies are necessarily unjust. We should be open to the possibility that some traditional forms of hierarchy were morally justified and they can serve as inspiration for thinking about just hierarchy in the modern world.

But which hierarchical relations are justified and why? In our view, it depends on the nature of the social relations and the social context. As a method, we are inspired by Michael Walzer's call for a pluralistic approach to justice.[34] There is no one principle of justice appropriate for all times and places. Our main argument is that different hierarchical principles ought to govern different kinds of social relations: What justifies hierarchy among intimates is different from what justifies hierarchy among citizens; what justifies hierarchy among citizens is different from what justifies hierarchy among countries; what justifies hierarchy among countries is different from what justifies hierarchies between humans and animals; and what justifies hierarchies between humans and animals is different from what justifies hierarchies between humans and (intelligent) machines. The sum total of our argument is that morally justified hierarchies can and should govern different spheres of our social lives, though these hierarchies will be very different from the unjust hierarchies that have governed much of our lives in the past. We support our arguments with a broad range of philosophical arguments and historical examples from different cultural traditions, as well as with extensive social scientific evidence and anecdotes from our personal experience. But we freely concede that our arguments are ultimately supported by the considered moral and political intuitions of readers sympathetic to our progressive conservative outlook. We have neither the desire nor the ability to persuade terrorists, white supremacists, antifeminists, misanthropes, narrow nationalists, warmongers, China-bashers, religious fundamentalists, climate-change deniers, die-hard conservatives, homophobes, and human carnivores with no moral qualms. Nor can we persuade leftists who dogmatically assert the value of equality in all realms of social life. Our hope is that progressive conservative thinkers will come to see the merits of just hierarchical relations in different kinds of social relations, not just because they are philosophically defensible, but also because they can help us think about solutions to the leading political challenges of our day.

We develop our argument in five separate chapters that correspond to five different forms of social relations and five different corresponding principles of hierarchy. These five hierarchical social relations are not meant to be exclusive, but they can and should govern much of our social lives. Chapter 1 focuses on relations between intimates that are characterized by emotions of love and care based on prolonged experience with face-to-face interaction. Much political theorizing, both in the West and (less so) in China, idealizes friendship between equals as the most desirable form of social relation. We do not dispute the desirability of friendship between equals, but we argue that an even higher form of social relation would include shifting hierarchies between intimates. Of course, hierarchies should not include violence, nor should they be fixed for eternity. But shifting hierarchies between lovers and family members are not just tolerable; they add much to the color and humor of social interaction. Even hierarchical relations between employers and housekeepers can be morally justified if they allow for role changes over time, though it might take a generation for such reversals to occur. Contemporary political theory does not provide the intellectual resources to develop our arguments on morally justifiable hierarchies between intimates, so we seek intellectual inspiration from ancient Chinese, Indian, and Greek thinkers.

In chapter 2, we turn to a discussion of just hierarchies between citizens—mainly strangers to one another—in modern large-scale political communities. It is a special challenge to justify hierarchies in political systems without voting mechanisms that (equally) empower citizens to change their rulers every few years. We argue that hierarchies between rulers and ruled in such communities are justified if the political system selects and promotes public officials with above-average ability and a willingness to serve the political community over and above their own private and family interests. We have the Chinese political context in mind, and we argue that this kind of ideal—what we call "political meritocracy"—helped to inspire the imperial political system in China's past and Chinese political reformers in the early twentieth century, and may help to justify the political system in China today. However, the meritocratic system needs to be accompanied by democratic mechanisms short of competitive elections at the top that allow citizens to show that they social equality in all spheres of social life. We hope that Western readers with a strong commitment to social equality will learn from this book if they seek to better understand China, but we do not expect that Western readers will be persuaded by many (or any) of our China-centered arguments.

That said, we do not entirely forsake the aspiration to universality. Default positions in favor of social equality are difficult to change, but they are not fixed for eternity. The field of business studies provides some evidence that biases in favor of social equality can be changed if need be: Managers from Western societies that value social equality can perform well if they adapt to the preference for social hierarchy in East Asian workplaces.[46] Nor is it hard to imagine political scenarios that allow for the implementation of morally justified hierarchies. In democratic countries, citizens are likely to become disillusioned with populist leaders who fail to deliver on extravagant promises ("Mexico will pay for the wall"), and there will be political pressure for meritocratic checks on populist excesses. So which parts of our book may seem more plausible, if not politically influential, to readers outside of China? Readers who share our progressive conservative perspective—an attachment to tradition and to progressive political causes—may more readily accept our fivefold division between the forms of morally justified hierarchies that inform different forms of social relations. The idea that different hierarchical principles should inform different social spheres— what works in the family may not work at the level of the state; what works between citizens may not work between states; what works between states may not work between human and animals; and what works between human and animals may not work between humans and machines—may resonate with the considered intuitions of people in all modern complex societies that allow for different forms of social hierarchy.

trust their rulers and provide a measure of accountability at different levels of government. In the Chinese context, however, there is a large gap between the ideal and the reality, and we argue that a judicious mixture of Confucian-style "soft power" combined with democratic openness, Maoist-style mass line, and Daoist-style skepticism about the whole political system can help to reinvigorate political meritocracy in China.

Chapter 3 discusses relations between states. Whereas relations between rulers and citizens in countries should be characterized first and foremost by actions that benefit the citizens, relations between countries need to be mutually beneficial for both countries. Notwithstanding lip service paid to the ideal of equality between sovereign states in the modern world, we argue that hierarchy between powerful and weaker states is the norm in international relations. Such hierarchical relations can be justified if they benefit both powerful and weaker states. We draw on a mixture of philosophy and history to argue that justifiable hierarchical relations can be characterized by either weak reciprocity—with both countries deriving instrumental benefits from hierarchical relations—or strong reciprocity—with decision makers in stronger and weaker states thinking of their relations from the perspective of both states, not just from the perspective of their own state. Strong reciprocity is more difficult to achieve, but it is more stable and long lasting than weak reciprocity. In terms of the future, we argue that an ideal of "one world, two hierarchical systems" may be appropriate for future forms of global order. Here too, modern theorizing is not sufficient, and we draw on the insights of ancient Indian and Chinese thinkers to make our points.

In chapter 4, we consider our relations with the animal kingdom. Throughout much of human history, most cultural and religious traditions—with some notable exceptions, such as

Daoism—have valued humans over animals. We argue that it is morally justifiable to posit a moral hierarchy with humans on top, but only if accompanied by the principle that humans should not be cruel to animals. But the principle of "subordination without cruelty" is not sufficient to spell out the kinds of obligations we owe to animals. We have different kinds of relations with different animals, and we owe the strongest obligations of care to animals with human-like traits and that contribute most to our well-being. In the case of animals bred for human consumption, we argue that such subordination is only justified if the animals are bred in humane conditions that are exceptionally rare in the modern world. We owe least to ugly animals that harm humans, but the principle of subordination without cruelty applies even in the case of the nastiest animals.

In chapter 5, we turn to perhaps the greatest challenge of our times: the need to maintain dominance over increasingly intelligent machines. We argue that machines can and should serve human interests—in that sense, they should be our slaves—and it is important to maintain such hierarchical relations of dominance. Here Marxism provides intellectual inspiration: The ideal of higher communism, with artificially intelligent machines doing socially necessary labor and humans freed to realize their creative essences, may be feasible several decades from now. But the state cannot and should not "wither away": A strong state will always be necessary to ensure that artificial intelligence does not invert the human-machine relation with humans on top and machines on the bottom. But worrisome science-fiction scenarios, with machines that seek to make humans into slaves, are challenges for the long term. In the short to medium term, we argue that Confucianism can help us to think of how to meet the challenge of artificial intelligence so that machines continue to serve human purposes.

The online appendix to our book is a joint statement—a kind of manifesto—signed by different political thinkers (including Daniel) in defense of the ideal of just hierarchy (https://press .princeton.edu/titles/30674.html). It is the product of a Berggruen Institute workshop on equality and hierarchy at Stanford University and was penned primarily by Julian Baggini. The manifesto helped to inspire this book (the detailed arguments were inspired mainly by conversations between Pei and Daniel over the past few years), and it also shows that there is potentially wide support for the ideal of just hierarchy in the modern world among people willing to question the received prejudice that social hierarchy is always a bad thing.

3. From China to the World

We expect that our defense of "just hierarchy" will resonate with the considered political intuitions of readers who share our progressive conservative perspective, with the implication that traditional hierarchies, properly reformed and updated for modern societies, can serve progressive political goals. But we recognize that the progressive conservative perspective may sound paradoxical to Western readers.[35] How can one be committed to both traditional values rooted in the past and to progressive values that point to a different (and better) way of doing things in the future? The mainstream narrative of modernity in Western societies is that traditional hierarchies expressed and institutionalized unjust values such as racism, sexism, and aristocratic privilege. Modern enlightened thinkers criticized traditional hierarchies and put forward strong arguments in favor of social equality and individual freedom that set the moral standard for future progress. There remains a large gap between the ideal and the reality, but hardly anybody openly argues for a return to the bad old days of rule by white men from aristocratic families. The default moral position, in the eyes of most Westerners, is a commitment to social equality and deep skepticism of the value of traditional hierarchies.

In China, it's a different (hi)story. Early Confucian thinkers criticized rulers on the grounds that they oppressed and impoverished ordinary people. In this sense they were political progressives. But rather than invoking new or future-oriented values as a moral standard for criticizing present-day injustices, they invoked standards from a golden age in the past that expressed morally desirable hierarchies in a harmonious society. The self-declared First Emperor of China, inspired mainly by Legalist ideas, implemented harsh policies that destroyed aristocratic privilege and built up a complex bureaucracy that expressed a commitment to social mobility based on merit. Subsequent imperial history was largely informed by Confucian commitments to both traditional social hierarchies and proto-socialist political ideals such as poverty reduction, equality of opportunity, and infrastructure projects designed to benefit the large majority of people. The imperial system broke down in 1911, and Western-influenced intellectuals blamed Confucian-style hierarchies for China's backwardness.[36] The tradition of antitraditionalism culminated in the Cultural Revolution, a disastrous attempt to abolish all forms of hierarchy from social life. Today, it is widely recognized by both government officials and leading intellectuals that China's way forward needs to draw on both conservative and progressive values: The default moral position often favors social hierarchy, and the question is how to make those hierarchies serve socially and politically progressive goals. In terms of our book, it means that our arguments in favor of morally justified social hierarchy might find a more ready audience in China and other East Asian societies influenced by Chinese culture such as Korea, Vietnam, and Japan.[37]

Needless to say, this somewhat crude sketch contrasting dominant political values of East Asia and the West overlooks important countercurrents.[38] But the default moral positions for or against social hierarchy continue to have great influence today. In Sweden, children often address all adults by their first (given) names,[39] the kind of lesson in social equality that would be inconceivable in China, not to mention societies such as Japan and South Korea that institutionalize social inequality by means of practices such as bowing at differential angles depending on a person's age and social status. In China, the supposedly egalitarian ideals of communism became transmuted into hierarchical social forms without much controversy: Even three-member party cells of the Chinese Communist Party are expected to appoint a leader in the form of a party secretary.[40] It would not be a gross simplification to assert that the norm of social equality has become the default moral position in almost all Western societies, which may not be the case in China and other Confucian-influenced East Asian societies. That's not to say Western societies have eliminated the need for hierarchy, but it takes a different form. In the United States, people feel valued by being treated as social equals, but the expression of superior status (and power) takes the form of wealth. It is fine to address Bill Gates by his first name, but it is also fine for the rich to separate themselves from the poor by means of living in gated communities. Libertarian arguments in defense of stark material inequality may be widely shared in the United States, but such views have almost no resonance in East Asian societies governed by hierarchical rituals that express differences in social status. Perhaps powerful members of East Asian societies need not rely on material wealth to show their superiority to the same extent.⁴¹ It seems that the powerful members of almost all complex societies need to express some form of hierarchy, and the choice comes down to Western-style economic hierarchy with a commitment to social equality versus East Asian–style social inequality with a commitment to economic equality.⁴² Such cultural differences are expressed in different languages: Although the most common word for hierarchy (*dengji* 等级) in Chinese is nearly as pejorative as the word "hierarchy" in English, it is easier to talk about morally justified social hierarchies in Chinese because the language has words such as *chaxu* (差序) that more readily lend themselves to the idea that not all social hierarchies are bad.⁴³ These differences are learned and reinforced in different childhood educational practices⁴⁴ and express different cognitive orientations.⁴⁵ Perhaps the cultural differences are most evident in the political sphere, and we do not expect that our arguments in favor of political meritocracy (chapter 2) or a China-led political hierarchy of states in East Asia (chapter 3) or for a strong Communist Party with the power to combat malevolent artificial intelligence (chapter 5) will have much persuasive power outside of China.

Cultural differences also matter when it comes to prioritizing different principles of hierarchy that inform different social spheres. Even if we agree that we can usefully posit the existence of different spheres informed by different principles of social hierarchy, we cannot assume that all these principles can be simultaneously implemented in some sort of harmonious way. That is, the successful implementation of a principle of hierarchy in one social sphere might conflict with, or undermine, the successful implementation of a principle of hierarchy in another sphere. It is entirely possible, for example, that a commitment to serving citizens by meritocratically selected rulers in a strong state (chapter 2) may conflict with the need to promote ties of strong reciprocity with weaker states (see chapter 3) since citizens of the stronger state may not be willing to share benefits with citizens of a weaker state. Even more worrisome, the commitment to ward off the potential challenge of "machine-masters" (chapter 5) may undermine the need for more democratic checks on the power of the state (chapter 2). In this case, which principle should have priority? Chinese thinkers steeped in a tradition of concern for *tianxia* ("All-under-heaven") may argue that the first principle should have ultimate priority because our very existence is at stake. But Americans are far less likely to accept the potential cost of a totalitarian state that leaves hardly any space for personal privacy or intimacy. If the license plate slogan in New Hampshire—LIVE FREE OR DIE—expresses a widely held view in that part of the world, then we do need to take seriously the question of how to prioritize the different hierarchical principles in cases of conflict, with potentially different rankings in different social contexts.

In short, we usually have the Chinese political context in mind. Some of our ideas may seem strange, if not morally outrageous, to people in societies far removed from the influence of Chinese culture. Our ideas originate *from* China: We support our arguments mainly (but not exclusively) with references to China's history and philosophical traditions such as Confucianism, Buddhism, Daoism, and stories from our personal experience living and working in China. And we write *for* China: We try to provide a coherent and rationally defensible account of the leading social and political ideas of China's public culture that can be used to critically evaluate the political reality in China. We do not mean to imply that our ideas only have validity in China. But what we say in favor of hierarchy needs to overcome a higher cultural hurdle in Western societies that strongly favor social equality in all spheres of social life. We hope that Western readers with a strong commitment to social equality will learn from this book if they seek to better understand China, but we do not expect that Western readers will be persuaded by many (or any) of our China-centered arguments.

That said, we do not entirely forsake the aspiration to universality. Default positions in favor of social equality are difficult to change, but they are not fixed for eternity. The field of business studies provides some evidence that biases in favor of social equality can be changed if need be: Managers from Western societies that value social equality can perform well if they adapt to the preference for social hierarchy in East Asian workplaces.[46] Nor is it hard to imagine political scenarios that allow for the implementation of morally justified hierarchies. In democratic countries, citizens are likely to become disillusioned with populist leaders who fail to deliver on extravagant promises ("Mexico will pay for the wall"), and there will be political pressure for meritocratic checks on populist excesses. So which parts of our book may seem more plausible, if not politically influential, to readers outside of China? Readers who share our progressive conservative perspective—an attachment to tradition and to progressive political causes—may more readily accept our fivefold division between the forms of morally justified hierarchies that inform different forms of social relations. The idea that different hierarchical principles should inform different social spheres— what works in the family may not work at the level of the state; what works between citizens may not work between states; what works between states may not work between human and animals; and what works between human and animals may not work between humans and machines—may resonate with the considered intuitions of people in all modern complex societies that allow for different forms of social hierarchy.

One important caveat: We do not mean to claim that there are completely separate principles justifying different kinds of social relations and that they all fit together in some seamless whole. For one thing, there may be social relations not discussed in depth in our book, such as the relation between employer and employee, teacher and student, commander and soldier, or religious leader and follower, that are informed by different principles of social hierarchy or that overlap with the principles discussed in this book. Social relations are not Platonic-like social spheres endowed with mystical autonomy: The social reality is far more complex in people's minds. Even if we agree, for example, with the argument (in chapter 1) that hierarchical relations between intimates are justified if they involve shifting roles, we might also agree that the principle invoked (in chapter 2) to justify hierarchies between rulers and citizens—those with power must care for those with less power—also applies to the relation between parents and children. Or else we might agree that the principle invoked (in chapter 3) to justify hierarchies between states—the relations should be mutually beneficial for both the powerful and the weaker parties—could also be invoked to justify our relations with pets (see chapter 4). The boundaries between social spheres and underlying hierarchical principles, in other words, are fluid. At best, we might be prepared to defend the claim that we identify different principles that *primarily* justify five different kinds of social relations in different social spheres in modern complex societies, but we do not mean to imply that those principles are exclusive or that the boundaries between social spheres are air-tight.

One final methodological point. We do not draw exclusively from Chinese history or philosophy to make our arguments. Our approach is closer to what Stephen Angle terms "rooted global philosophy: that is, taking one's own philosophical tradition as a point of departure, but being open to stimulus from other philosophical frameworks as one strives to make progress (as progress is measured from one's own, current vantage point)."[47] So we draw on ancient Greek and Indian philosophy and contemporary French and Anglophone philosophy, as well as social science studies and the history of societies outside of East Asia, if they help to strengthen our arguments. As a general rule, the more we draw on international intellectual resources, the more exportable our arguments. What we say about shifting roles that justify "nighttime hierarchies" (chapter 1) or the hierarchical principle of "subordination with care" that justifies our relations with domesticated animals (chapter 4) draw heavily on intellectual resources outside the Chinese context and may have more persuasive power at the global level.

To summarize, our arguments are mainly rooted in the Chinese context and will have more persuasive power in that context. But the progressive conservative perspective is not absent from modern societies outside of China, and some of our arguments in favor of morally justified hierarchies and the boundaries between them may also persuade readers in those societies. At the end of the day, it's up to the reader to decide which arguments are persuasive and which ones aren't. There is one universal value that we wholeheartedly endorse: the need to read with a critical eye. We encourage readers to always ask themselves what's wrong with our arguments and to think how they can be improved (or rejected). Our book is preliminary—to be more positive, it is the first systematic exploration of just hierarchies in modern societies—and we look forward to critical comments that will allow somebody else to write a better book on the topic. ☺

1

Just Hierarchy between Intimates

ON THE IMPORTANCE
OF SHIFTING ROLES

Confucius said: "In ancient times, the enlightened rulers
served their fathers with filial piety, and therefore, served the
heavens with clarity. They served their mothers with filial
piety, and therefore served the earth with insight. When the
young follow their elders, relations between higher and lower
ranking people are well regulated."

—*CLASSIC OF FILIAL PIETY, CH. 16*

WE SPEND MUCH of our time interacting with our intimates.
Lovers, family members, and friends give meaning to life, and
it's almost unbearable to imagine a life (only) with strangers. Yet
it takes only a moment's thought to realize that we do not often
interact with intimates on a basis of equality. A parent can freely
criticize a five-year-old child who does the wrong thing, and
while the parent should not be immune to criticism, nobody
thinks the child is an equal when it comes to judgments about
what kind of life to lead. In China and other countries that value

filial piety, it's common for adult children to defer to the views of an experienced and wise elderly parent. Lovers have intimate nighttime rituals of power displays that accompany (if not contribute to) the highest forms of passion and compassion, and it's not the business of the state to intervene in such matters. In countries such as India and China, longtime housekeepers are not social equals but they can be loved and treated almost like family members.

That's not to say hierarchies between intimates are always justified. We oppose any relation that involves involuntary physical violence toward another person, no matter how loved the recipient, and we will not try to argue for such relations. We do want to argue that nonviolent hierarchies can be justified if they involve shifting roles. What makes the caste system so morally repugnant is that hierarchical social roles are fixed for eternity.[1] But there's nothing wrong with shifting hierarchies. More than that, changing hierarchical roles between family members and lovers add much to the color and humor of social interaction. Just as it's hard to imagine a life (only) with strangers, so it's hard to imagine a life with intimates that prescribe equal treatment at all times. Nothing would be more boring! The one exception is the interaction between friends. It's the one social relation that does assume equal status, except in extreme circumstances that deviate from the default position of social equality. Even conceptions of friendship that allow for differences in personalities prescribe comparable treatment, without any differences of power or ranking. Friends are both moral and social equals. Perhaps that's why prominent thinkers in both Western and Chinese traditions have valued friendship as the highest form of social relation. But are they correct to do so?

1. Relations with Friends

In the waning years of the Ming dynasty, an influential Confucian scholar and radical social critic, He Xinyin (1517–1579), spent two years trying to avoid arrest by the imperial court. He was helped by his close friends, but the authorities caught up with him, and he died in prison in the fall of 1579. His last wish was to be buried next to his close friend, the scholar Cheng Xu. This "final act" created an uproar at the time because it contravened the Confucian norm that the dead should be buried next to their relatives, thus earning He the epithet "crazy Confucian" (狂儒). In his own mind, however, He was not "crazy"; rather, he aimed to provide a morally desirable interpretation of Confucian ethics. He did not reject the five cardinal interpersonal relations of Confucian ethics: between parent and child, there should be affection; between sovereign and minister, righteousness; between husband and wife, attention to their separate functions; between old and young, proper order; and between friends, fidelity. But whereas traditional Confucians valued the first four hierarchical relations—with special value on the parent and child relation as the most "natural" and the starting point for all the others[2]—He argued that the relation between friends, founded on equality, was the highest form of social relation, which should serve as the standard for structuring other human relations. Even seemingly hierarchical relations should be infused with the spirit of egalitarian friendship. For example, the relation between teacher and student should be a mutual learning process, with both interacting as equal teachers (相师) and friends (相友).[3] And what made the sage rulers of the past so successful is that they interacted with ministers, younger siblings, and even their own children as though they were equal friends and teachers of each other.[4] He traces the origin of his theory to Confucius himself: "Only friendship could assemble all the talented under Heaven. . . . That's why the Confucian orthodoxy could be traced back to Confucius in the Spring and Autumn period. . . . The Dao of friendship was revealed to Confucius by Heaven, so that he could reach the highest good."[5] But He was an innovator, not just a transmitter. He was the first Confucian thinker to argue that friendship is the highest form of social relation and that friends should be both teachers and students learning equally from each other. And he was the first to argue that the ideal of equal friendship should serve as the standard to evaluate other social relations.[6] That's why contemporary scholars praise He as the pioneer of the "Chinese enlightenment."[7] But is the ideal of equality between friends really the highest—most desirable— form of social relation?

He's idealization of friendship is more common in the history of Western philosophy. A recent book on the relation friendship between the eighteenth-century thinkers David Hume and Adam Smith paints a moving depiction of their deep friendship. Both Hume and Smith valued friendship as the highest social good: Hume held that "friendship is the chief joy of human life," and Smith proclaimed that the esteem and affection of one's friends constitutes "the chief part of human happiness."[8] More-over, their own friendship constituted the very highest form of friendship, with two friends motivated by virtue and excellence: "a stable, enduring, reciprocal bond that arises not just from serv-ing one another's interests or from taking pleasure in one anoth-er's company, but also from shared pursuit of a noble end: in this case, philosophical understanding."[9] In the Western tradition, the archetype of ideal friendship can be traced to Aristotle. In Aris-totle's view, there are numerous kinds of friendship in the real ethical world. He used the word "friendship" as a metaphor to discuss (1) the relation in a family, for example friendship between parents and children and between husband and wife; (2) unequal relations, such as the friendship between rulers and subjects and between elders and the young; and (3) friendship in a community, for example, friendship among travel companions and friendship among soldiers.[10] But the different kinds of friendship are not equal in moral worth. Some are motivated by utility, some by pleasure, and the highest and rarest form—such as the friendship between Hume and Smith (Aristotle himself does not offer any examples)—is motivated by virtue or excellence, with two equals who seek the ethical life in common: "Perfect friendship is the friendship between good people and similar in virtue."[11] For both Aristotle and He, the highest human relation is characterized by two equal friends sincerely committed to the other's good and who jointly partake of the ethical life.[12]

The sixteenth-century philosopher Michel de Montaigne endorsed Aristotle's ideal of friendship between equals, but he denied that other forms of friendship are possible. For Montaigne, two people who are not equals cannot be friends: Given the big gap between father and son, for example, it is more appropriate for the son to respect his father.[13] Montaigne also reversed Aristotle's view that love, as an excess of emotion, has a character similar to perfect friendship. For Aristotle, love is as extreme as "perfect friendship," and it is equally rare: One cannot have many true friends, just as it is only possible to love one person.[14] For Montaigne, however, love is inferior to friendship. The intensity of love and friendship is not the same, and the "*chaleur douce*" of friendship is more long lasting than the strong erotic passion of love: "As soon as love enters the territory of friendship (where wills work together, that is), it languishes and grows faint. To enjoy it is to lose it: its end is in the body and therefore subject to satiety. Friendship on the contrary is enjoyed in proportion to our desire: since it is a matter of the mind, with our souls being purified by practicing it, it can spring forth, be nourished and grow only when enjoyed."[15] Friends are soulmates, not body-mates, and body and soul should be kept separate. That's not to say soul-mates can't share their souls, just as lovers share their bodies. For Montaigne, the highest form of friendship involves the merging of souls, so that equality becomes sameness. Montaigne was speaking from personal experience with his dear friend Étienne de la Boétie: "I know his soul as well as mine. . . . Everything actually being in common between [us]—wills, thoughts, judgments, good, wives, children, honor, and life—and [our] relationship being that of one soul in two bodies, according to Aristotle's very apt definition, [we] can neither lend nor give anything to each other."[16]

From a normative point of view, however, the merging of souls is questionable. The twentieth-century French philosopher Emmanuel Levinas agrees with Montaigne that friendship between equals can merge into sameness: "My friend and I, we define each other by the relation between us. He is a soul mate, another me (alter ego). Oreste and Pylade are a related pair. The pair of friendship is like the marble and the groove where it rests. According to the mythology of Aristophanes in Plato's *Symposium*, being double [*l'être double*] would rather be friendship than love. In friendship, every dynamic is absent: friends possess each other."[17] True friends speak with one voice, one heart and one mind, and experience the same emotions: "In his position, I feel my friend's emotions again through my own sentiment, feel happy for his happiness, and mourned for his pain."[18] Like the person who has found the other half in the mythology of Aristophanes, two friends do not have separate identities. But for Levinas, sameness is not something to be celebrated. Quite the opposite. When "friends possess each other," they exercise power ("puissance") over each other, which can easily lead to violence.

Here Levinas inverts Montaigne. Far from being inferior to the relation of friendship, the relation of love (what Levinas terms "eros") is superior precisely because it preserves a distance between self and other that can never be conquered. As long as the distance exists, the relation between self and other can never be a relation of power. Lovers do not seek to complete each other, but to deepen their relation.[19]

So who's right? We can accept Levinas's critique of Montaigne's ideal: Identities should not be merged. Who wants to be controlled by a "friend" who claims to think the same things and experience the same emotions as me? But good friends need not—and should not—have the same identity (if anything, lovers are more likely to merge their identities in unhealthy ways). They can be equal but different, each helping the other to improve her- or himself and to flourish in her/his own distinctive way. We can also accept Levinas's point that lovers should maintain their separate identities. But here too, he goes too far. What would it mean to completely do away with power relations? Drawing on a wide range of findings from the animal world and human societies, the cultural anthropologist Christopher Boehm argues that humans have an innate tendency to dominate as well as an innate tendency to resent being dominated.[20] Hierarchy is a ubiquitous feature of human relations, and it is unrealistic to wish it away. That's not to say we can't have the equality of friendship, but any social relation also needs to make room for hierarchy, and the task is to distinguish between good and bad forms of hierarchy and to promote social relations that have more of the former.

In any case, it makes sense to consult one's own experience, which might ultimately have more persuasive power than whatever great philosophers have said in the past. It seems hard to object to the ideal of friendship between equals. And we can learn from friends precisely because they are different. But it doesn't take long to come to the conclusion that friendship is not the highest or most ideal social relation in many people's minds: Think of the "goodbye" letter from a boyfriend (or girlfriend) to another with the devastating line, "let's just be friends." This kind of letter implies that loving intimacy is even more valued than ideal forms of friendship.[21] But what makes the relation between loving intimates so great? Here's our take. Lovers are usually more other-regarding: they typically care and sacrifice for each other more than ordinary (or even extraordinary) friends. A less obvious—but equally important—reason is that lovers can treat each other as equal friends in the day, while incorporating night-time hierarchical relations that add color and joy to their lives.[22] But what kind of nighttime hierarchical relations between intimates are morally justified? Let's explore this in the next section.

2. Relations with Lovers

The relation between lovers is the most intimate form of social relation, because it involves not just intellectual, moral, and spiritual love, but also physical love. And the highest form of love between intimates involves mutual surrender, when both "sides" let go of the defenses that normally accompany social interaction. The lovers let their emotions flow freely, caressing and kissing without constraint, and let their selves merge to the point of self-annihilation. Even the usual rules of self-love prescribed by evolution do not apply to the highest form of love between intimates: a lover can sincerely wish for a child that looks and thinks just like her intimate (a thought that would never occur to animals).

But love between intimates is also extremely dangerous. The lover, who has surrendered his or her self to the other without any mode of self-protection, is particularly vulnerable to abuses of power, not just physical but also emotional and social. And much of the interaction between lovers takes place when nobody is watching, in the privacy of the bedroom. Hence it is doubly important that hierarchies between lovers are not fixed and allow for changes over time. We worry most about hierarchies between intimates that mirror and reinforce hierarchies in other spheres of social life. Just about every society in human history has been informed by strongly hierarchical social relations that express patriarchal dominance over women. Men hold unjust power over women in work and politics. Feminists have long argued that patriarchal relations within the home have negative implications for women outside the home: Women's opportunities in the "public" sphere will be limited so long as women do a large share of child-rearing and housework in the "private" sphere (hence the slogan, "the personal is the political"). When it comes to hiring and promotion, most bosses will prefer (male) workers who can (supposedly) devote themselves to the job without worrying too much about family obligations.[23] Less discussed (and admittedly, more speculative) is the view that "nighttime hierarchies" between lovers may exacerbate these negative effects on women. If "private" sexual relations between lovers (whether married or not) are characterized by male dominance—with the male on top and playing the more active role—it's hard to believe that the psychological effects of male dominance won't be transferred to other realms of social interaction, including daytime interaction between lovers.

But what if the female is the dominant partner in nighttime hierarchies? Surely that can challenge patriarchy in other realms of social life? Not so sure. In Japan and South Korea, patriarchal power relations outside the home are far more deeply entrenched than in mainland China (whatever we think of the Chinese

revolution, one of its effects has been to equalize gender relations compared to other large-scale Confucian-influenced societies in East Asia). Japanese and Korean wives typically control
the family finances, but such practices can reinforce patriarchal power relations outside the home. For one thing, the expectation that women "run the home" means that employers
are less likely to consider female job candidates who (employers
think) won't be able to devote themselves wholly to work. And
the fact that women have power at home may also limit their
aspirations outside the home. If women get some satisfaction
from controlling (most of) what happens in the home, they
may have less desire to push for equalizing power relations outside the home. We do not know what happens in the bedrooms of Japan and South Korea, but a similar mechanism
may be at work if the woman is the dominant partner in nighttime hierarchies. If women can get a high degree of satisfaction
from being in control and exercising power during sexual intimate relations, it may also limit their desire to challenge patriarchal relations in the worlds of work and politics.

In short, nighttime hierarchies are problematic from a femi-
nist point of view when lovers habituate themselves to unchang-
ing habits of dominance and subordination, even if the woman
is the dominant partner. The solution may then seem obvious:
Intimate lovers should change their hierarchies over time. Nighttime hierarchies need to be unfrozen and roles (ex)changed
over time. But what can be done to realize this ideal? We do not
think it's a matter for state intervention or legal regulation. However much we may object to the social and political effects of
nighttime hierarchies, we agree with former Canadian prime
minister Pierre Trudeau (current prime minister Justin Trudeau's
father) that the state has no business in the bedrooms of the nation. But it's still something to worry about, and politically

progressive intimate lovers can learn techniques designed to unfreeze nighttime hierarchies.

The ancient Chinese classic *The Records of Rites*, written between the fourth and second centuries BCE,[24] offers an intriguing example of a role reversal. In a ritual that follows the death of a ruler, the ruler's son becomes the new ruler, who then performs the sacrifices to his deceased father, while an impersonator plays the role of the role of the deceased, receiving sacrifices from the living. What's interesting is that the living ruler's own son—who is normally supposed to be deferential and subordinate to his father—would play the part of the impersonator for the ghost of his grandfather (the ruler's deceased father):

> Now, according to the way of sacrificing, the grandson acted as the impersonator of the king's father. He who was made to act as the impersonator was the son of the one who made the sacrifice. The father faced north and served him. By means of this, he made clear the way of a son serving his father. This is the relation of father and son.[25]

The stated goal of the ritual, Michael Puett explains, "is to inculcate in each performer the proper dispositions that should hold in the relationship between father and son."[26] The learning takes place by means of role reversals, with the ruler behaving as a proper son to his own son, and the son as the honored elder receiving sacrifices from his own father. The assumption is that the participants will learn to think and act from the perspectives of those who are on the other ends of the hierarchies in everyday life—the powerful will learn to think and feel from the perspective of the subordinate, and vice versa—hence softening the anger, jealousy, and resentment that normally accompany fixed and rigid hierarchies. Carnivals in European cultures serve a similar function, with role reversals and impersonations that release participants from the fixed and rigid hierarchies of everyday life. Some corporations today rely on such role reversals—the CEO takes a job at the lower levels for a day or two—in order to break down the deleterious effects of fixed hierarchies and encourage a certain degree of empathy and understanding for those on the other ends of hierarchies. Intimate lovers can also engage in such role reversals of nighttime hierarchies, with the active, relatively powerful lover playing the part of the subordinate, and vice versa.

The Kamasutra

But role reversals between intimates cannot be one-off games. The changes must be frequent to be long-lasting, and they must be relatively spontaneous, almost unselfconsciously performed during acts of passion and compassion, to truly engage with the emotions of the participants. Here the Indian classic the *Kamasutra* offers particularly valuable insights. The *Kamasutra*, or the *Treatise on Pleasure,* composed in the third century CE, is the world's most influential textbook on erotic love. It is famous today largely because of its explicit sexual content (often accompanied by pictures added by translators and publishers to boost sales), but "it is a book about the art of living—about finding a partner, committing adultery, living as or with a courtesan, using drugs—and also about the positions in sexual intercourse."[27] The book opens with a brief discussion of the three aims of human life valued in ancient Hindu texts—religion/moral duty (*dharma*), power/material success (*artha*), and pleasure/love/ desire (*kama*). When the three aims compete, "each is more important than the one that follows,"[28] but the rest of the book is a discussion of *kama* (the least important). The book is a joy to read, not just because, as Wendy Doniger explains, it "reveals attitudes to women's education and sexual freedom, and non-judgmental views of homosexual acts, that are strikingly more liberal than those of other texts in ancient India—or, in many cases, contemporary India,"[29] but also because of its somewhat lighthearted, almost cynical tone. The text is largely written from a male point of view, to maximize the man's pleasure. But parts of the text are explicitly directed at women: "Scholars [pedants] say: 'Since females cannot grasp texts, it is useless to teach women this text.' Vatsyayana [author of the *Kamasutra*] says: But women understand the practice, and the practice is based on the text. . . . And there are also women whose understanding has been sharpened by the text: courtesans and the daughters of kings and state ministers."[30]

The *Kamasutra* views sex "as a form of quarrelling, because the very essence of desire is argument, and its character is competitive."[31] But the power struggles are told from both male and female perspectives. It is clearly sympathetic to women, particularly when they suffer from inadequate lovers. The amusing discussion of how a courtesan can get rid of an unwanted (male) lover is worth quoting at length:

> She does for him what he does not want, and she does repeatedly what he has criticized. She curls her lip and stamps on the ground with her foot. She talks about things he does not know about. She shows no amazement, but only contempt, for the things he does know about. She punctures his pride. She has affairs with men who are superior to him. She ignores him. She criticizes men who have the same faults. And she stalls when they are alone together. She is upset by the things he does for her when they are making love. She does not offer him her mouth. She keeps him away from between her legs. She is disgusted by wounds made by nails or teeth. When he

tries to hug her, she repels him by making a "needle" with her arms. Her limbs remain motionless. She crosses her thighs. She wants only to sleep. When she sees that he is exhausted, she urges him on. She laughs at him when he cannot do it, and she shows no pleasure when he can. When she notices that he is aroused, even in the daytime, she goes out to be with a crowd.

She intentionally distorts the meaning of what he says. She laughs when he has not made a joke, and when he has made a joke, she laughs about something else. When he is talking, she looks at her entourage with sidelong glances and slaps them. And when she had interrupted his story, she tells other stories. She talks in public about the bad habits and vices that he cannot give up. Through a servant girl, she insults him where he is vulnerable. She does not see him when he comes to her. She asks for things that should not be asked for.[32]

One wonders if the author speaks from his own unhappy experience, but what's certain is that women (not just courtesans) are provided with an exhaustive list of tips for puncturing the male ego.

The *Kamasutra*'s account of shifting roles in nighttime power games helps us think about morally justifiable hierarchies between intimate lovers.[33] The text pays lip service to conventional (patriarchal) ideas of gender: "By his physical nature, the man is the active agent and the young woman is the passive locus. . . . The man is aroused by the thought, 'I am taking her,' the young woman by the thought, 'I am being taken by him.' . . . A man's natural talent is his roughness and ferocity; a woman's is her lack of power and her suffering, self-denial and weakness."[34] Intimate lovers, however, can (and should) deviate from these norms: "Their passion and a particular technique may sometimes lead them to exchange roles, but not for very long."[35] Women need to take the lead in initiating such role reversals:

> When she sees that the man has become exhausted by continuous repetition, but that his passion is still not quenched, she may, with his permission, roll him under her and give him some help by playing the man's part herself. Or she can do it out of her own desire to do something she has only imagined doing, or to satisfy the man's erotic curiosity. To play the man's part, when he is inside her, she gets on top and puts him underneath her. . . . She says, "You threw me down, and now I am throwing you down in return," laughing and threatening him and hitting him. And at the same time, she indicates that she is embarrassed and exhausted and wishes to stop.[36]

The power games and role reversals may get out of hand, especially for the "powerful" man: "Whatever wound a man inflicts on a woman, even when she tries to restrain him and cannot bear it, she should do that very thing to him twice as hard. . . . She grabs him by the hair and bends down his face and drinks from his mouth; she pounces on him and bites him here and there, crazed with passion."[37] But role reversals can help the man learn about his lover's needs: "Even when a sensual woman covers up her own feelings and hides her signals, she unveils her own feelings completely when her passion drives her to get on top. A man can learn everything—a woman's personality, what sort of sex excites her—from the ways she moves on top."[38] Role reversals contribute to the diversity that sustains passion: "For even passion demands variety. And it is through variety that partners inspire passion in one another."[39] Hence, role reversals can help to stabilize long-term relationships between intimate lovers: "When two people behave in this way with modesty and concern for one another's feelings, their love will never wane, not even in one hundred years."[40] Conversely (by implication), fixed hierarchies between intimates undermine love and mutual concern, and kill off passion.

It might seem strange, perhaps even counterproductive, to advocate detailed techniques for role reversals with the aim of deepening passion between intimates. The more one thinks about such techniques, the less unbridled the passion. But humans are not animals when it comes to sex: "Scholars [pedants] say . . . Since even animals manage to have sex by themselves, and since it goes on all the time, it should not be handled with the help of a text." Vatsyayana says: "Because a man and a woman depend on one another in sex, it requires a method, and this method is learned from the *Kamasutra*. The mating of animals, by contrast, is not based on any method: because they are fenced in, they mate only when the females are in their fertile season and until they achieve their goal, and they act without thinking about it first."[41] The method involves role reversals so that both lovers learn more about each other: "The best alliance plays the game so that both sides taste one another's happiness and treat one another as unique individuals."[42] Once the techniques are learned, they can be unselfconsciously performed, with frequent changes of roles motivated by passion rather than the desire to perfect a technique: "The territory of the texts extends only in so far as men have dull appetites; but when the wheel of sexual ecstasy is in full motion, there is no textbook at all, and no order."[43] The *Kamasutra* aims to make itself obsolete in the long term. Intimate lovers will have learned the techniques that contribute to lasting passion, including frequent role reversals in nighttime hierarchies, and then unselfconsciously apply those techniques without need of any text.

In short, what's distinctive about morally justifiable hierarchies between intimate lovers is not just that they involve role reversals, but that, ideally, those role reversals are frequently and unselfconsciously applied in the midst of passionate embraces. Not only will these role reversals contribute to the diversity and empathy that help sustain passion over the long term, but they can also help to challenge the patriarchal relations that typically characterize other spheres of social and political life (both in ancient India and in the contemporary world). Let us now turn to other forms of morally justifiable hierarchies between intimates. These also involve role reversals, but with longer time spans in family-based hierarchies, and even longer time spans in hierarchical relations with housekeepers.

3. Relations with Family Members

The idea that there is a hierarchy between elders and younger people is central to Chinese culture. Mencius (known as Mengzi in Chinese) and Xunzi, for example, notwithstanding totally different starting points about human nature, both agree that there should be age-based hierarchical rankings between people.[44] Throughout Chinese history, this idea was institutionalized by means of laws and informal norms that empowered the elderly in a variety of economic, social, and political ways.[45] Still today, the Chinese political system is structured so as to ensure that top decision makers have decades of experience: since 1989, nobody under fifty has assumed positions in the Standing Committee of the Politburo.

Age-based hierarchies are rooted in the idea of filial piety (孝). We ought to revere elderly members of the family, and then extend that reverence to elderly people as a whole.[46] Note that filial piety does not simply refer to the idea that children ought to (generally speaking) obey their parents. Every known society accepts a hierarchy between parents and children. Parents, due to superior knowledge and morality, have power over children, but parents are supposed to use that power to help children develop into flourishing adults. What happens when children reach adulthood, say, around eighteen years of age? In the West, the assumption is that adult children and their parents are then equals, and hierarchical relationships are no longer justified. In China, the assumption is that parents continue to have some form of unequal authority over adult children and adult children are supposed to serve their elderly parents. They are not equals, even when both are adults.

What justifies age-based hierarchies between adult children and elderly parents? Confucian thinkers often invoke the argument that filial piety is distinctive to human beings.[47] Animals, like humans, often care for their children, but they typically do not care for their elderly. Even if the claim that filial piety is distinctively human is correct, we still need to justify a move from descriptive fact to normative injunction (the ability to develop intricate means of inflicting pain may also be distinctive to humans, but it's not a good thing). It's also worth asking what, if anything, hinges on the descriptive fact: If filial piety is a good thing, and if it turns out that some animals do care for their elderly, we should praise those animals rather than give up our commitment to filial piety.[48] So Mencius's argument can't be the whole, or even the main, story. Another argument is more recent: Filial piety is central to Chinese culture and if we care about maintaining Chinese culture, we should care about maintaining filial piety.[49] But clearly filial piety has changed over the years. The days when elderly parents controlled the family income and property are long gone; now, adult children typically support their elderly parents. And fewer and fewer people live with their elderly parents. Elderly parents have far less say in family decisions compared to families in imperial China. Clearly elderly parents are becoming more and more disempowered. Whether this trend is good or bad is a separate question, and we need more arguments to defend the claim that (what's left of) age-based hierarchies should be maintained, if not reinforced in the future.

What, then, are the arguments in favor of age-based hierarchies between adult children and their parents? There are six arguments that, together, constitute a strong case for age-based hierarchies. The first argument, more closely tied to the family, invokes the value of reciprocity. Our parents cared for us when we were children, and adult children have an obligation to care for elderly parents when they are older and frail. That seems fair. In the West, adult children often serve their parents, but it's viewed as a matter of choice. Not in China: Adult children must serve their adult parents, a norm that is often reinforced by legal means.[50] Yes, the state will need to play a greater role in providing elderly care in the future (given that many single children need to support two adult parents), but the ideal of providing care for elderly parents is not likely to lose its normative force in the foreseeable future. And some social practices that express reverence for the elderly are still widely followed in China: For example, adult parents typically get first dibs at communal dishes at the family table. Still, the idea that we have an obligation to serve our parents does not necessarily translate into an argument that elderly parents should assume leadership roles in hierarchical relations with their adult children: We also have an obligation to care for our house pets, but the pets are not our masters. So we need more arguments to justify age-based hierarchies within the family.

The second argument invokes the value of learning from experience. This argument is not distinctive to humans. Female red deer, for example, do not fight for dominance of the herd. The leaders are usually older, and they lead because the followers "recognize the experience that comes with age."[51] But humans can do even better: They can consciously commit themselves to learning in a way that broadens their intellectual horizons. Learning is a never-ending process of accumulating knowledge: As Confucius put it, "A person who is constantly aware of what has yet to be learned and who, from month to month, does not forget what has been learned, can be said to truly love learning" (19.5).[52] Since reading and studying are time-consuming processes, the elderly are more likely to have had the time to read and study with a view to improving their lives. Hence, adult children need to defer to the intellectual judgments of elderly parents, other things being equal. But other things are rarely equal. In disciplines such as mathematics or physics, the best intellectual work is often done by thinkers in their twenties or thirties. And today, youngsters often need to teach elderly parents (and grandparents) about uses of modern gadgets essential for navigating the social and virtual worlds. Whatever intellectual authority the elderly may have had in the past has been eroded by the youthful virtuosos of Silicon Valley and Shenzhen. So we need still more arguments for age-based hierarchies within the family.

The third argument invokes the value of emotional intelligence.[53] From a Confucian standpoint, it seems obvious that emotional intelligence—meaning social skills such as self-awareness, self-regulation, and the ability to understand others—normally increases over time. As we age, we experience different roles (such as dealing with bosses, colleagues, and subordinates in the workplace) and deepen our experience in particular roles (a community organizer with ten years' experience should be more effective than a brand-new organizer), and thus we increase our ability to understand and cooperate with different kinds of people for the purpose of achieving desired ends, so long as we maintain the quest for self-improvement and our desire for social interaction. As it turns out, scientific research bears out this Confucian insight: "One thing is certain: Emotional intelligence increases with age."[54] Fredda Blanchard-Field's research compares the way young adults and older adults respond to situations of stress and "her results show that older adults are more socially astute than younger people when it comes to sizing up an emotionally conflicting situation. They are better able to make decisions that preserve an interpersonal relationship. . . . And she has found that as we grow older, we grow more emotionally supple—we are able to adjust to changing situations on the basis of our emotional intelligence and prior experience, and therefore make better decisions (on average) than do young people."[55] Other research shows that older adults seem particularly good at quickly letting go of negative emotions because they value social relationships more than the ego satisfaction that comes from rupturing them.[56] In short, we have good reason to empower elderly parents in the family context— to give them more voice, and let them decide in moments of emotional conflict—because they are more likely to have superior social skills. On the other hand, a sociopath with superior social skills can "read" people and manipulate them for immoral purposes more effectively than an incompetent and insensitive person. So we need still more arguments to justify age-based hierarchies within the family.

The fourth argument invokes the value of moral growth.[57] One of the most widely quoted sayings from The Analects of Confucius is the brief account Confucius gives of his own life: "At fifteen, I set my mind upon learning; at thirty, I took my stance; at forty, I was no longer perplexed; at fifty, I realized the 'ways of the universe'; at sixty, my ear was attuned; at seventy, I followed my heart's desire without overstepping the boundaries" (2.4). In contemporary China, the saying has been somewhat distorted: for example, thirty-year-olds take Confucius to be saying that they should be established in their careers. But Confucius himself is tracing his own progress of moral growth: His capacity for moral judgment improves, and he can act better, morally speaking. Why does he think morality improves with age? The text is not so clear, but one reason for believing that the elderly have greater capacity for moral judgment is that they are less likely to be enslaved by sexual desire. Confucius notes that he can give free rein to his heart's desires at the age of seventy, meaning that there is less of a conflict between what he wants to do and what he should do. Why would Confucius say that? Elsewhere in the *Analects*, Confucius notes despairingly that he "has yet to meet anybody who is fonder of virtue than of sex" (15.13). But Confucius is addressing his own students, and he may not say the same thing to an older crowd. That is, as sexual desire diminishes with age, there may be less conflict between the desire for sex and the desire to do good. This is not to imply that the desire for sex is entirely extinguished for elderly people, but it is easier to control and subordinate to moral principles (compared to male adolescents!). That said, the phenomena of sexual abuse and harassment do not, sadly, have an age limit, so we need still more arguments to defend age-based hierarchies among adult family members.

The fifth argument invokes the value of economic equality. Zhang Taisu argues that seniority-based social hierarchies in early modern China served to safeguard remarkably persistent socioeconomic equality. Qing and Republican property institutions often gave greater economic protection to the poorer segments of society than comparable institutions in early modern England: "the comparatively 'egalitarian' tendencies of Qing and Republican property institutions stemmed from the different ways Chinese and English rural communities allocated social status and rank. Hierarchical 'Confucian' kinship networks dominated social and economic life in most Chinese villages. Within these networks, an individual's status and rank depended, in large part, on his age and generational seniority, rather than personal wealth. This allowed many low-income households to enjoy status and rank highly disproportionate to their wealth."[58] In other words, age-based hierarchies at the family and village levels actually promote economic hierarchy at the societal level: If people are given power because of their age, not their wealth, the state is less likely to enact policies that benefit the rich, and the overall effect will be to equalize the distribution of wealth (relative to societies that do not empower the elderly). Of course, such policies were based on patriarchal assumptions that we reject today: Only the elderly men had substantial power in traditional China. But a gerontocracy without gender bias would still equalize wealth, so in principle it's a good idea to strive to empower elderly men and women in the family and the local community (assuming that we worry about radical inequalities of wealth distribution). The bigger problem is practical. Zhang objects to the "socialist" road to economic equality on the grounds that it involves too much coercion in the form of strong state regulation and aggressive wealth distribution from the top. Empowering the elderly in families and local communities could achieve the same end without nearly as much coercion. But it's hard to imagine the Chinese Communist Party reviving such "feudal" practices from the past. And it's even harder to imagine such pro-gerontocracy reforms in democratic Western societies without a history of empowering the elderly. It is abstractly conceivable that, say, extra votes for the elderly could mitigate the power of wealth in the United States,[59] but the rest of the society is almost certain to object strongly to such measures.

The sixth argument invokes the value of harmony. Harmony in the Confucian sense of peaceful order and respect for diversity depends on the idea that there is a "decider" who has the authority to make the final call in cases of conflict.[60] Without a "decider," conflicts that cannot be solved by love and peace are likely to spin out of control, as factions fight for victory, thus undermining social harmony. In politics, the "decider" would be, ideally, a public official with superior ability and virtue and a proven track record of good performance. Families are not (and should not be) meritocracies to the same extent: They are supposed to be run on love and informal norms, and it would be absurd to subject elderly parents to a battery of tests before they can assume positions of power in the family.[61] But it does make sense to empower the family member who is (1) owed thanks due to previous love-infused work on behalf of the family, (2) more likely to have the most knowledge, (3) more likely to have superior emotional intelligence, and (4) more likely to be in control of his or her sexual urges. Elder members of the family are more likely to instantiate these *desiderata* (counter-examples may readily come to mind, but it's a question of tendencies). Empowering family elders is also likely to promote more economic equality in the political community. Hence, on balance, there is a good case for empowering the elderly members of the family, with the consequence that adult children typically need to defer to their elderly parents in cases of conflict.

Still, we need to reiterate our opposition to hierarchies that become frozen and impervious to change. So do we need to worry about fossilized age-based hierarchies in the family? Not really. For one thing, younger family members on the bottom of the family hierarchy can and should criticize powerful elders who commit moral wrongs. In the Confucian tradition, even young children have an obligation to criticize parents who commit moral wrongs, though it must be done in an appropriate context. The Qing dynasty classic "Rules for Students" (弟子规)—still widely taught in China's primary schools today—suggests three steps to the young child: first, use persuasion; if that doesn't work, then wait until the parent is happy, and try again; if that doesn't work, then try weeping and wailing, working on the parent's emotions; and if that doesn't work, then the child needs to accept the parent's will (including the use of physical punishment, which we do not endorse).[62] There is still inequality between parent and child—these conditions of critique do not apply in the case of the parent criticizing the child who commits a wrong—but clearly there is no injunction of blind obedience on the part of the child. Plus, it makes sense to say that the child needs to obey the parent at the end of the day, if none of the tactics are successful (other than extreme situations, the final option should not be to run away or change families). But does it make sense to say that adult children have to defer to elderly parents in cases of conflict? In the past, elderly Chinese parents arranged the marriages of their adult children, and few young people want to bring back those days. But it's still common, and widely accepted, for elderly parents in China to set up meetings with potential marriage mates for their adult children, and there is also an expectation that parents be consulted before the marriage deal is closed. Being the "decider" does not necessarily mean exercising veto power in all aspects of family life. It might mean that adult children have an obligation to consult elderly parents when they make decisions, whereas elderly parents do not have the same obligation to consult with adult children (e.g., if elderly parents decide to get remarried). Such unequal social practices may seem dubious in the West, but they are taken for granted in Confucian-influenced China.

Another reason not to worry is that roles in age-based hierarchies, by definition, change over time. The child will become
an adult, and then an elder, who will eventually have the same
authority over adult children that her or his own parents had.[63]
In that sense, age-based hierarchies are fundamentally different,
and more legitimate, than race- or gender-based hierarchies that
are fixed for eternity. Moreover, the hierarchy between adult
children and elderly parents often ends up with a complete role
reversal. Beyond a certain age, the elderly parent often loses the
capacity to make decisions due to physical and mental dete-
rioration. In the case of Alzheimer's patients, elderly parents
literally regress over time, to the point that they become like
helpless babies. At that point, there is a complete role *reversal*,
with adult children taking charge of the decision making.[64]
In traditional China, most people did not live long enough
for Alzheimer's to manifest itself, which may help to explain
why role reversal in the family was rarely discussed in ancient
texts. And in the future, we will hopefully discover ways of
slowing down, if not eliminating, cognitive and physical decline.
But for the moment, we can expect that the hierarchical relation between adult children and their elderly parents will often
be characterized by complete role reversals over the long term.

We do not mean to imply that the traditional Confucian justifications for hierarchical relations between family members
should serve as the standard for assessing hierarchical relations
in the family today. Traditional Confucians also tried to justify
a hierarchical relation between wife and husband that is morally
indefensible from a progressive perspective.[65] We do think that
Confucian-inspired justifications for age-based family hierarchies, properly adjusted to contemporary norms of gender
equality, are still relevant today. But there may be an additional
worry. If age-based hierarchies are justified, does it follow that

we should revive the Confucian-style hierarchical bond between elder and younger brother, modernized so that it refers to the hierarchical bond between elder and younger sibling, regardless of gender? Our response is that it depends on the age gap. Daniel is eleven months older than his younger sister, and while he occasionally invokes the Confucian need for deference to elder siblings, he has not been effective in asserting his authority over his sister. Perhaps the age gap with his sister is too small for the advantages of age difference to kick in. But the elder sibling may have a legitimate claim to unequal power in the family if there is, say, a twenty-year gap between the two siblings. An elder sibling with decades of experience is more likely to have superior knowledge, social skills, and virtue, and is owed thanks if he or she cared for the younger one. So age-based hierarchies in the family may be extended beyond the child-parent relation, but only if the age gap approximates the same age gap as that between child and parent.

In short, age-based hierarchies between family members, like hierarchical relations between intimates, may involve role changes if not complete reversals: That's key to their moral legitimacy. The age-based role changes do occur, though at a much slower pace than role changes between intimate lovers. As we will see, however, one role change between hierarchical intimates takes even longer: the change in the relation between employer and housekeeper.

4. Relations with Housekeepers

Perhaps the most infamous argument in the history of (Western) political theory is Aristotle's defense of slavery: Some people are born to be slaves, therefore slavery is justified. How can someone so smart—the genius among geniuses—get it so wrong?

Well, for one thing, he recognizes that slavery would not be necessary in a world of advanced technology: "if every instrument
could accomplish its own work, obeying or anticipating the will
of others, like the statue of Daedalus, or the tripods of Hepha-
estus, which, says the poet, 'of their own accord entered the assembly of the Gods,' if in like manner, the shuttle would weave
and the plectrum the lyres, chief workmen would not want servants, nor masters slaves."[66] Clearly slavery is not something to
celebrate. Aristotle couldn't foresee the development of modern
machines and artificial intelligence, but he'd probably be over-
joyed by the prospects that all humans, including slaves, could
potentially be freed from the need to engage in menial labor (see
chapter 5). Karl Marx did foresee a world where machines do all
the drudge labor—he called it higher communism—but he also
recognized that exploitation of workers is a necessary evil until
we get to that stage.

Aristotle also argues that the use of raw power cannot justify
slavery: "There is slavery by convention as well as by nature. The
convention is a sort of agreement—the convention by which
whatever is taken in war is supposed to belong to the victor. But
this right many jurists impeach, as they would an orator who
brought forward an unconstitutional measure: they detest the
notion that, because one man has the power of doing violence
and is superior in brute strength, another shall be his slave and
subject."[67] Enslaving prisoners of war is not a justification for
slavery, particularly if the war is unjust: "Others, clinging as they
think simply to a principle of justice (for convention is a sort of
justice), assume that slavery in accordance with the custom of
war is just, but at the same time deny this. For what if the cause
of war be unjust?"[68] Nor can success in war justify enslaving the
children of prisoners of war: "And again, no one would ever say
that he is a slave who is unworthy to be a slave. Were this the case,

men of the highest rank would be slaves and the children of slaves if they or their parents chanced to be taken captive and sold."[69] In short, Aristotle's defense of slavery is somewhat half-hearted. It only applies in a world where human intelligence is necessary to provide the necessities of life, and it does not apply to "worthy" people who happen to have been enslaved in war, nor does it extend to the next generation.

So what exactly is Aristotle's argument for "natural" slavery? He says: "For that some should rule and others be ruled is a thing not only necessary, but expedient, from the hour of their birth, some are marked out for subjection, others for rule."[70] Even if true, however, that is not a sufficient argument for slavery. Mencius, writing around the same time, made a similar argument: "Some labor with their minds, and some labor with their strength. Those who labor with their minds rule others, and those who labor with their strength are ruled by others. Those who are ruled by others feed people, and those who rule people are fed by others."[71] This passage was frequently cited in defense of social hierarchies in traditional China, but never as a justification for slavery. It referred to the idea that those with superior intelligence (and virtue) should be put in positions of power, but their obligation is to serve the others with compassion (a notion that is largely absent from ancient Greek thought), not to exploit them.[72] Those who are ruled have an obligation to work the fields to feed the rest of society, but certainly not to serve rulers *qua* slaves.[73] So Aristotle needs another argument to defend "natural" slavery. His argument depends on a strong distinction between the soul and the body and their respective roles:

A living creature consists in the first place of soul and body, and of the two, the one is by nature the ruler and the other the subject . . . the soul rules the body with a despotic rule, whereas the intellect rules the appetites with a constitutional and royal rule. And it is clear that the rule of the soul over the body, and of the mind and the rational element over the passionate, is natural and expedient; whereas the equality of the two or the rule of the inferior is always hurtful. . . . When then there is such a difference as that between soul and body, or between men and animals (as in the case of those whose business is to use their body, and who can do nothing better), the lower sort are by nature slaves, and it is better for them as for all inferiors that that should be under the rule of a master. For he who can be, and therefore is, another's, and he who participates in reason enough to apprehend, but not to have, is a slave by nature. Whereas the lower animals cannot even apprehend reason, they obey their passions.[74]

The first thing to note is that Aristotle's argument has no purchase in a philosophical culture that rejects, or doesn't work with, the soul-body distinction. In ancient China, it was a nonissue: the "soul" hadn't been invented as a concept and, more generally, there was no mind-body dichotomy (the word 心 *xin* in classical Chinese is usually translated as "heart-mind"). Even assuming the distinction between soul and body, however, the boundaries are unclear. Aristotle argues that rulers are those whose (rational) souls rule over their (passionate) bodies. Slaves are the opposite, but they have the ability to apprehend the dictates of reason (unlike animals). But how can we confidently identify those with worthy souls, given that, as Aristotle admits, "the beauty of the body is seen, whereas the beauty of the soul is not seen"?[75] And how can we be sure that those with not-so-beautiful souls cannot be improved with education? Aristotle seemed to have recognized the limits of his own argument at the end of his life: "in Aristotle's will, the only genuinely personal

document from his pen that we possess . . . we find Aristotle free-
ing his slaves, an unnecessary and generous gesture for a man
of his time."[76] If Aristotle had persuaded himself that some
people were born to be slaves, why did he go out of his way to
grant freedom to his own slaves?

What's interesting for our purposes is that Aristotle's argument for slaves is made in the context of a discussion about
household management and the work of slaves includes "cook-
ery and similar menial arts."[77] And here there may be more par-
allels with other cultures. In ancient China, for example, there
was not a formal system of slavery, but housekeepers were often
bound to households for life, and had to serve their masters in
ways that may not have been so different in substance than Aristotle's household slaves. However, housekeepers were also
bound within a Confucian ethical system that often mitigated the
worst abuses of domestic servitude.[78] A basic assumption of
Confucian ethics is that the moral life is possible only in the context of particularistic personal ties. For the general population,
the most important relationship by far is the family. It is by fulfilling our responsibilities to family members that we learn about
and practice morality (for Aristotle, in contrast, the good life lies
outside the home). The value of caring for children is widely
shared in other cultures, but Confucianism places special emphasis on reverence for elderly parents (aka filial piety). Moreover,
reverence for elders is not simply a matter of providing material
comfort. As Confucius put it, "It is the attitude that matters. If
young people merely offer their services when there is work to
do, or let their elders drink and eat when there is wine and food,
how could this be [sufficient for] filial piety?"[79] We need to serve
our parents, and other family members, with love.[80] Morality
within the immediate, blood-related family, however, is not sufficient. In Confucianism, there is a firm distinction between

family insiders and nonfamily outsiders, but the concept of family is relatively flexible, and family-like concern and care are supposed to be extended to others. Mencius explicitly asks us to "Treat the aged of our own family in a manner befitting their venerable age and extend this treatment to aged of other families; treat our own young in a manner befitting tender age and extend this treatment to the young of other families."[81] One mechanism for extending such care is to treat housekeepers, or longtime domestic servants, almost like family members. In China's past, family-like labels and norms were often extended to housekeepers and longtime housekeepers were sometimes treated with care and respect that went beyond treatment accorded to family members.[82]

Of course, housekeepers in China's past were not really family members. Even in the best cases when they were treated with family-like love and care and their full personalities could develop and shine, housekeepers were still bound to the home as domestic servants and were not included in the family line. There was always a sharp differentiation of roles between family members and housekeepers. Today, fortunately, the practice of bound housekeepers has been relegated to China's "feudal" past. But the system of extending family-like love and care still shapes interactions between employers and housekeepers in contemporary China. Day care and nursing-home systems are relatively undeveloped, even in wealthy Chinese cities. People worry that strangers entrusted with caring duties won't show the right "attitude," hence the reluctance to commit one's children and elderly parents to state (or private) institutions. It's much better for family members to provide care for other needy family members, and if that's not possible, to hire somebody to provide personal care in the home. So middle-class and upper-class families often hire housekeepers to help with caring duties. In mainland Chinese cities, they typically hire migrant workers from the impoverished countryside, and in Hong Kong, they hire migrant workers from the Philippines, Indonesia, and other relatively poor Southeast Asian countries. In the best cases, the housekeepers are treated like family members: It is not uncommon for children of employers in modern China to refer to housekeepers as "auntie" (阿姨). One recent study provides a good example of family-like treatment by a Chinese employer in Hong Kong. A Filipina housekeeper (aka domestic helper or domestic worker) valued her employer's parents because she was treated as the daughter they never had. The ties between the employee and the employer's family were based on mutual concern and caring, not simply fairness and respect (which was more characteristic of the "good" Western employers): They watched TV together, engaged in mutual teasing, and the employer showed sincere concern for the housekeeper's family in the Philippines. Interviews with other housekeepers in Hong Kong revealed similar reactions. One housekeeper praised her former boss in Singapore for her use of affectionate family-like appellations and for including her in weekend family outings. Another housekeeper was made the godmother of her employer's child, and they would go to church together. Such cases of family-like treatment are rare in Hong Kong, but they may be more common in mainland China where there are fewer linguistic and cultural barriers between employer and housekeeper. Here too, however, it's worth keeping in mind that housekeepers are not really (or wholly) treated like family members. The hope is that treating housekeepers like family members increases the likelihood that they will care for the employer's family members with love and care, but even in the best of cases the roles of housekeeper and family member are kept distinct.[83]

We will simply assume that blatantly unfair treatment of housekeepers—paying unreasonably low salaries, forcing them to work unreasonably long hours, verbal abuse, not to mention physical violence and sexual exploitation—is bad and should be curbed to the extent possible.[84] It is difficult for the state to monitor such abuses because interaction with housekeepers takes place in the "privacy" of the home, but it can enforce strict punishments for publicly exposed abuses. Other forces for decency in society, including family members of immoral employers, can and should help to rein in such abuses. But what if the housekeepers are paid well above the market rates, given substantial time off, and treated with both respect and family-like care, and both employers and housekeepers are satisfied with such arrangements? There is still a clear hierarchy, but perhaps it's justified. Before we go that route, we need to recognize that the life of a housekeeper should never be viewed as more than a necessary evil, similar to Aristotle's slaves and Marx's proletarians in technologically undeveloped society. Housekeepers do it for the money, and overseas domestic workers and migrant workers from the countryside are deprived of interaction with their own family members while they live and work for their employers, so the system is a double evil. Ideally, no one would be forced to travel long distances and be deprived of key family relations simply to make a decent living. In the long term, assuming an optimistic scenario, economic necessity will no longer influence what people do. We will have overcome the problem of global poverty, robots will help to care for needy family members, and nobody will need to take jobs as housekeepers.

But in the meantime, we need to consider under what conditions the intimate hierarchy between employer and housekeeper—the least intimate of intimate hierarchies, but intimate nonetheless because interactions take place inside the home and (in the best cases) can take the form of family-like relations—can be justified from a moral point of view in a nonideal world. At minimum, the employer needs to refrain from all forms of mistreatment and humiliation. But beyond that, the employer has a positive obligation to treat the housekeeper with respect and, especially in cultures that value extending family-like treatment, like a family member.[85] And beyond that, it depends on the nature of the housekeeper. Here we can (re)turn to Aristotle's (otherwise horrible) argument about "natural" slaves for inspiration. Consider two kinds of housekeepers:

Housekeeper 1 is a Beijing-born resident. She is not poor but works as a housekeeper to earn some extra funds for her family. She is neither intelligent nor ambitious, lacks any sense of humor, does her job in a rigid but effective way, and her interactions with her employer and family members are kept to a bare minimum.

Housekeeper 2 is from the Chinese countryside. She is from a poor family and could not even finish primary school due to economic constraints. But she goes to Beijing of her own accord with an impressive desire to improve herself. She learns how to drive and works as a "black car" (illegal taxi) driver because only those with a Beijing household registration (*hukou*) can work as taxi drivers. She is hired by a Beijing-based employer without any formal contract. The employer hires her as a driver and a cook (she is an excellent and highly imaginative cook) and all-around helper. The employer's son is very fond of the housekeeper, and vice versa. They eat meals as a family, discuss intimate family affairs, and the housekeeper's moral insights help to smooth out family conflicts. The employer is impressed by the intelligence and drive of her housekeeper and gives her books on the Chinese classics, which the housekeeper devours in her spare time. Meanwhile, the housekeeper saves enough to buy two apartments in the Beijing suburbs, which she rents out to other migrant workers for a healthy profit. After eleven years, the housekeeper leaves the employer's family, taking up a new job as a teacher in an informal school that teaches the classics to young children.

In the case of Housekeeper 1, the employer has no obligation other than to refrain from committing moral harms, treating the housekeeper with respect, and making some effort, however minimal, at family-like treatment. But Housekeeper 2 is different. Clearly she would have done well had she been given decent opportunities to flourish, and she ended up as a housekeeper only because she had the bad luck of being born in a very poor family. So the employer, even though it's against her long-term interests (because it's difficult to find an honest, loving, and intelligent housekeeper), has an obligation, if she has any sense of decency, to plan for a role change: to provide the resources and opportunities for Housekeeper 2 to assume another role that provides more respect and income and allows for full flourishing of her natural talent. The employer, to go back to Aristotle's example, must plan for the freedom of the housekeeper. But what about a role exchange between employer and housekeeper, with each taking the role of the other? That may be asking too much of the employer because it's hard to imagine any employer of housekeepers being willingly downgraded to the role of housekeeper, except in extraordinary times such as revolution or economic collapse.[86] But the employer needs to be prepared for the possibility of complete role reversals in the next generation. If the employer gives birth to a dull-witted child or a child with talents not valued by the marketplace, and

Housekeeper 2 gives birth to an intelligent and energetic child with economically valuable skills, then it is possible, and fair, that Housekeeper 2's child could end up as the employer of her employer's child.[87] Role reversals between employers and housekeepers take longer than reversals in other intimate hierarchies, but if they do occur we can conclude that the intimate hierarchical relation between employer and housekeeper is morally justified.

A similar dynamic of shifting roles helped to justify direct democracy in ancient Athens, with rulers and ruled taking turns. Today, most citizens in liberal democracies do not take an active part in ruling, but the voting system provides a form of equality, giving citizens the right to change their rulers every few years in free and fair elections. How might it be possible to justify hierarchical relations in large modern societies without a voting mechanism? Here we need to consider a different dynamic.

2

Just Hierarchy between Citizens

ON THE IMPORTANCE OF SERVICE

If we gather as a group for a meal, then it is the concern of
everyone, and we naturally call for everyone's idea and decide
by majority vote. . . . If we regard the aim of life as satisfying the
desires of human beings, and regard the aim of politics as
fulfilling everyone's desires, we have to decide by majority
vote. . . . However, if we regard life as a process of moral
improvement, rather than the satisfaction of ordinary desires, it
would be different. . . . It means we all need to pay respect to our
teachers and to continuously ask for advice from people, and we
would naturally choose the leadership of a minority [with above
average ability and virtue], and not decide by majority vote.

—LIANG SHUMING, *RURAL
RECONSTRUCTION THEORY*, 1937

RELATIONS BETWEEN INTIMATES are characterized by
strong emotions of love and care based on prolonged experience
with face-to-face interaction. In the previous chapter, we argued
that hierarchies between intimates can be justified if they are

characterized by changing roles that break down ossified power relations. In small political communities composed of citizens who trust and know one another, the justification for hierarchies may be similar. In ancient Athens, for example, a few thousand (male) citizens took turns as ruled and rulers via such mechanisms as regular rotation and sortition meant to equalize chances of holding office in the executive branch that set the agenda for the assembly, deliberation and voting on policies in frequent meetings in the assembly, popular law courts with juries selected by lot, as well as local governments that modeled their organization and deliberations upon that of the city and created strong bonds of solidarity among citizens.[1] While the whole system was founded on morally unjustified hierarchies (slaves and women did most of the socially necessary labor), the hierarchical relation between citizens was morally justified because every citizen had an opportunity to rule at some point in his life and no one could dominate others for extended periods of time.

In large-scale political communities composed mainly of strangers, however, most people will not have the opportunity to rule over others. In China, for example, it is simply not feasible for 1.4 billion citizens to take turns ruling and being ruled. Any attempt to implement an Athenian-type democracy would be a recipe for chaos in huge political communities of this sort. So political hierarchies composed of rulers who exercise power over large groups of strangers for extended periods need a different justification. The most influential alternative for large-scale political communities has been indirect representative democracy in the form of voting in free and fair periodic elections. Although most citizens won't have a chance to rule in large political communities, at least they have the equal opportunity to select, and deselect, their rulers every few years. Social science studies that draw pessimistic conclusions about the rationality

of voters,[2] as well as the election of demagogic leaders with au-
thoritarian inclinations in the mold of United States president
Donald Trump, Turkish president Recep Tayyip Erdogan, and
Hungarian prime minister Victor Orban, have cast doubt on the
moral legitimacy and long-term viability of "actually existing"
electoral democracy. Political theorists such as Yves Sintomer
and Wang Shaoguang have written persuasive works arguing that
modernized interpretations of sortition are more likely (compared to elections) to realize democratic values in both small-
and large-scale political communities.[3] But let us leave aside
these debates. We would like to focus the discussion on the possibility of justifying hierarchies between rulers and citizens in
large-scale political communities (such as China) that do not use
periodic elections to select rulers.

1. Justifying Hierarchical Political Rule in the Chinese Context

The most obvious justification for hierarchy in large communities is efficiency. According to historian Niall Ferguson, "The
crucial incentive that favored hierarchical order was that it made
the exercise of power more efficient: centralized control in the
hands of the 'big man' eliminated or at least reduced time-
consuming arguments about what to do, which might at any
time escalate into internecine conflict."[4] Moreover, the larger the
political community, the more efficiency considerations favor
centralized, hierarchical rule in the hands of the few: "The core
lesson of classical political theory was that power should be hierarchically structured and that power naturally became more
concentrated in fewer hands the larger a political unit became."[5]
Chinese political history bears out this insight. Pre-imperial
China was characterized by fierce military competition between

small warring states. After the late fifth century BCE, however, "a synergism of the necessities of war, the power of the state, and Legalist ideology [a philosophy that justifies heavy-handed state power and harsh punishments to secure social order] held sway: increasingly the power of ferocious warfare favored those states that were more instrumental in organization and action; the warfare of ordinances imposed by the Legalists enhanced state capacity to harness aristocratic power and exact resources from the population; and the states that were more able to act instrumentally by more thoroughly implementing Legalist regulations were likely to triumph in the fierce military competition."[6] The Qin state proved to be most efficient at centralizing power and promoting a ruthlessly efficient military meritocracy (soldiers were promoted based on the number of decapitated heads of enemy soldiers),[7] and the Qin successfully unified China under the one-man rule of Qin Shi Huang, the self-proclaimed First Emperor of Qin.

But we have to ask: What's the point of pursing efficiency in politics? Private companies prioritize efficiency because it's necessary to maintain an edge *vis-à-vis* other profit-seeking competitors, but states need to have a moral mission and efficiency can be justified only if it helps with that mission. The core justification for the state—whether the state is governed by one ruler, a few rulers, or many rulers, as Aristotle famously argued in *Politics* III.7—is that policies must benefit the ruled (rather than the rulers). Hence, the pursuit of efficiency cannot be morally justified if it conflicts with that aim. The Qin empire lasted for only fifteen years—the shortest-lived major dynasty in Chinese history—precisely because it lost sight of the state's moral mission. In line with Legalist thinking, Emperor Qin Shi Huang aimed to increase state power and employed ruthlessly efficient means for that end. He developed the world's first sophisticated bureaucracy, unified the Chinese script, and built an advanced transportation and communication system, but still went down in history as cruel dictator.

The next major dynasty—the Han—found the normative solution that lasted for nearly two thousand years. The Han dynasty was still willing to use ruthless officials: *The Book of Han* (汉书) even had a special chapter titled "Biography of Cruel Officials."[8] But the Han adopted the political thought of Confucianism—a philosophy that justifies using compassionate politics to benefit the people—as the governing ideology. Qin Shi Huang was famous for burning books and burying Confucian scholars. By contrast, Emperor Wu Di adopted Dong Zhongshu's (179–104 BCE) interpretation of Confucian thought to educate the people and train officials with a unified Confucian ideology. Emperor Wu Di did not forsake the use of Legalist-style severe laws and punishments—five out of fourteen ministers during his fifty-year reign were executed—but he used Confucian thought to provide legitimacy for his rule, setting the dynamic for subsequent imperial political history. As Zhao Dingxin explains,

In the Confucian-Legalist state, the emperors accepted Confucianism as the ruling ideology and subjected themselves to the control of a Confucian bureaucracy, while Confucian scholars both in and out of the bureaucracy supported the regime and supplied meritocratically selected officials who administered the country using an amalgam of Confucian ethics and Legalist regulations and techniques. This symbiotic relationship between the ruling house and Confucian scholars gave birth to what is by premodern standards a powerful political system—a system so resilient and adaptive that it survived numerous challenges and persisted up until the Republican Revolution in 1911.[9]

The Legalist legacy is less evident because Legalism largely disappeared from official discourse for nearly two thousand years—there were no card-carrying Legalists from the Han dynasty until Mao's invocation of Legalism in the Cultural Revolution. But Legalist ideas were employed to improve the state's capacity and ensure administrative efficiency. Whatever the official rhetoric, the political system often relied on a Legalist standard for the selection of competent public officials, namely, the selection of officials with the ability to carry out strong and effective execution and the willingness to use brute power to solve problems for the emperor. But the Legalists were not overly concerned with the question of whether the aim itself was just or moral. So Confucianism set the aim of politics—to persuade the emperor to "Rule for All" (天下为公). Confucians favored the selection and promotion of public officials who could grasp the moral Way (道), implement benevolent policies that benefit the people, and protect civilians from cruel policies. The Chinese term for political meritocracy—the selection and promotion of public officials with superior (Confucian-style) virtue and (Legalist-style) ability (贤能政治)—well captures the ideal of the public official with an ability to grasp practical issues with the aim of efficiently implementing the principle of "Rule for All." In reality, however, Legalism and Confucianism often pulled in different directions. From a Legalist perspective, Confucians often selected exemplary men who lacked the ability to deal with practical politics and efficient administration. From a Confucian perspective, Legalists often selected capable villains with no desire for justice or morality. Legalists deferred to the emperor's wishes as the final court of appeal, whereas Confucians relied on the moral Way to evaluate the status quo, with a responsibility to admonish the emperor who implemented immoral policies. Legalists cynically dismissed the possibility of morality and criticized Confucians as hypocrites who sowed political chaos, whereas Confucians doubted that a political system could survive for long without a moral foundation. This kind of dynamic between Confucianism and Legalism, as we will see, continues to influence Chinese politics today.

Whatever its internal tensions, what we can term the "Legalist Confucian" ideal of political meritocracy not only informed Chinese politics for over two thousand years,[10] more surprisingly, it has also inspired political reform in China over the past four decades or so. A typical trope in the Western media is that there has been substantial economic reform in China, but no political reform. But that's because electoral democracy at the top is viewed as the only standard for what counts as political reform. If we set aside this dogma, it's obvious that the Chinese political system has undergone substantial political reform over the past few decades, and the main difference is that there has been a serious effort to (re)establish political meritocracy.[11] The country was primed for rule at the top by meritocratically selected officials following a disastrous experience with radical populism and arbitrary dictatorship in the Cultural Revolution, and China's leaders could reestablish elements of its meritocratic tradition, such as the selection of leaders based on examination and promotion based on performance evaluations at lower levels of government—almost the same system, in form (but not content) that shaped the political system in much of Chinese imperial history—without much controversy. And since then, political meritocracy has inspired political reform at higher levels of government, with more emphasis on education, examinations, and political experience at lower levels of government. There remains a large gap between the ideal and the practice, but the underlying motivation for political reform is still the ideal of political meritocracy.

From a normative perspective, the ideal of political meritocracy is most compelling at higher levels of government in large-scale political communities. The reason is that it is much more difficult to rule and manage huge and incredibly diverse countries such as China, and it is not helpful to compare China with small, relatively homogenous countries endowed with plentiful natural resources.[12] Moreover, at higher levels of government of large countries, problems are complex and often impact many sectors of society, the rest of the world, and future generations. In large countries, political success is more likely with leaders who have political experience at lower levels of government and a good record of performance. Electoral democracy may be appropriate for small countries or at lower levels of government of large countries; even if things go wrong—say, too much populism and small-minded navel-gazing at the cost of neglecting long-term planning and concern for future generations and the rest of the world—it's not the end of the world. But it may well be the end of the world if things go drastically wrong at the top of big and powerful countries. The policies of leaders at the top of huge political communities shape the lives of hundreds of millions people, including future generations and the rest of the world. Hence, the ideal of political meritocracy is more appropriate to assess the higher levels of political systems of large countries like China.

Of course, the ideal of political meritocracy would be a nonstarter in political communities where there is widespread aversion to the idea that is important to select and promote public officials with superior ability and virtue. In such communities, the best (or least bad) option might be to seek to improve the quality of decision making of elected politicians, whatever the theoretical and practical challenges. In China, however, political meritocracy has been consistently supported by political reformers since the turn of the twentieth century. As Liang Shuming put it, "if we regard life as a process of moral improvement, rather than the satisfaction of ordinary desires ... we would naturally choose the leadership of a minority [with above-average ability and virtue] and not decide by majority vote."[13] More recently, survey results consistently show widespread support for the ideal of political meritocracy (aka "guardianship discourse").[14] The ideal is widely shared, much more so than the ideal of selecting leaders by means of elections. And the ideal of political meritocracy is also widely used to evaluate the political system. Corruption became such a big issue in the popular mind at least partly because of the expectation that meritocratically selected leaders are supposed to have superior virtue. But the ideal of political meritocracy may not be an appropriate standard for evaluating political progress (and regress) in societies where the ideal is not typically used by the people to evaluate their political leaders.[15]

In short, the ideal of political meritocracy is an appropriate standard for assessing political progress and regress at higher levels of government in China because the ideal has been central to Chinese political culture, it has inspired political reform over the past few decades, it is appropriate for large-scale political communities, and it is endorsed by the vast majority of the people. These reasons may be particular to the Chinese context, but there are also more general reasons to support the ideal of political meritocracy in the modern world. For one thing, political meritocracy, with its emphasis on high-quality leaders with wide and diverse political experience and a good track record of responding and adapting to changing circumstances, may be particularly appropriate in a time of fast technological change and unpredictable global shocks. It may have made sense for the eighteenth-century founders of the United States to enshrine a rigid constitutional system because they could be quite sure that society would not change much over the course of the next few decades. It was more important to fix a good political system than to allow for an ever-evolving political system that aims to select and promote different kinds of high-quality leaders appropriate for different times. But today, the only thing we can predict about the next few decades is that there will be radical changes to our current way of life,[16] and the quality of leaders will matter even more than the quality of our political institutions (more precisely, our political institutions should be designed with the aim of selecting and promoting leaders with wide and diverse political experience and a good track record of responding and adapting to changing circumstances).

That said, the ideal of political meritocracy needs to be complemented by democratic values and practices. In China, the ideal of democracy is widely deployed in both official and unofficial political discourse.[17] So perhaps the most compelling argument for political meritocracy is that it is compatible with most democratic values and practices, unlike, say, fascism or communist totalitarianism. Political meritocracy can and should be complemented by such democratic practices as sortition, referenda and elections, consultation and deliberation, as well as the freedom of speech. That's not to say all political goods go together. Political meritocracy is not compatible with competitive elections at the top because electoral democracy for top leaders would undermine the advantages of a system that aims to select and promote leaders with experience, ability, and virtue: An elected leader without any political experience (such as Donald Trump) could rise to the top and make many beginner's mistakes, an elected leader would have to spend valuable time raising funds and giving the same speech over and over again instead of thinking about policy, and an elected leader would be more constrained by short-term electoral considerations at the cost of long-term planning for the good of the political community and the rest of the world.

Is Transparency Desirable?

There may also be limits to transparency in a political system that values political meritocracy. In China, the powerful organization department—like the human resources department of the world's largest communist organization—has the task of selecting and promoting public officials with above-average ability and virtue. The organization department has become somewhat more transparent of late: Its criteria for selection and promotion (and demotion) are more transparent, and it has put on mock interviews for visiting dignitaries from abroad, showing how candidates are selected in the interview process, though without naming real people. But we still do not have any clear idea of why some candidates get promoted over others who appear to be equally well qualified. Daniel put this question to leaders of the organization department in Shanxi in June 2017. Shanxi was perhaps China's most corrupt province, and Daniel was invited for a government-led tour. The point of the tour was probably to show that the organization department had successfully replaced corrupt cadres with a new group of clean and hard-working leaders. Daniel took this opportunity to ask a leader of the province's organization department why the selection process can't be more transparent. If their leaders are so great, surely it would help them make the case, both to fellow Chinese and to the outside world, to show that the leadership selection process is, in fact, rigorous and meritocratic. The organization department leader asked how professors select candidates in academia. Daniel replied that the relevant department establishes a committee that aims to select the best candidates, and committee members deliberate among themselves. The leader asked if the deliberations are open. Daniel replied of course not: Open deliberations would set constraints on what's said, nor would it be fair to the candidates who are not selected. The leader smiled and said that "the same goes for us." And he explained that the organization department—one of the most selective and prestigious departments in the Chinese political system—selects candidates partly according to their ability to keep secrets. So while political meritocracy may be compatible with most democratic values and practices, we should just accept that lack of transparency is an inevitable cost of any organization that aims to select the best candidates. It's true not just of the Chinese Communist Party (CCP) and academia, but also of Goldman Sachs and the Catholic Church. That's not to say we can't hope for more transparency in the Chinese political system—the words and actions of emperors were tracked by official court historians for posterity in imperial China, and today we can imagine, say, video recordings of the deliberations of CCP leaders to be released fifty years from now. But full transparency is both unrealistic and unfair to the "losers" in the Chinese political system.[18]

To sum up. The hierarchical ideal of political meritocracy is an appropriate standard by which to assess the political reality at higher levels of government in China for a mixture of contextual and general reasons. The practical question is how to close the gap between the ideal and the reality. On the one hand, it means thinking about how best to maximize the advantages of the system. But any defense of political meritocracy also needs to address the question of how to minimize the disadvantages of the system. If the disadvantages are so great as to outweigh the advantages, then we can no longer be confident that political meritocracy should be used to assess the political reality in China (or elsewhere). The next three sections will discuss problems associated with any attempt to implement political meritocracy: (1) Rulers chosen on the basis of superior ability are likely to abuse their power; (2) political hierarchies may become frozen and undermine the ideal of equal opportunity; and (3) it is difficult to legitimize the system to those outside the power structure.[19] Given that electoral democracy at the top is neither desirable nor feasible in China, we will ask if it is possible to address these problems without democratic elections.

2. Is It Possible to Limit Political Power without Competitive Elections?

At the end of the day, what justifies political meritocracy (or any other political system) is that its leaders serve the people. This means, at minimum, that the leaders should respect the basic human rights of people: prohibitions against slavery, genocide, murder, torture, prolonged arbitrary detention, and systematic racial discrimination, as well as the idea that all citizens should be equal before the law in criminal cases. Leaders should also strive to secure the basic material needs of the people, such the right to food and decent health care. Such values are shared at the level of principle in most modern societies, including contemporary China. Of course, political leaders should do much more than respect basic human rights, but political priorities will vary with the circumstances (e.g., there is stronger need to place emphasis on poverty reduction at very low levels of GDP per capita and more need to combat environmental degradation once the country becomes wealthier). What won't vary, however, is the need for leaders who put the interests of the political community above their own or family interests. Such requirements are most obvious in the case of the military: Soldiers are expected to be prepared to die if necessary to protect the political community. But political leaders who systematically misuse power for their own or family benefit will also undermine the well-being of the community. Leaders need not be totally self-sacrificing or virtuous, but a degree of virtue is indispensable: Without any desire to serve the public, a political leader can put his or her ability to disastrous uses. So a political meritocracy must aim to select and promote leaders who are likely to use their power to serve the public.

The problem, of course, is that meritocratically selected leaders have few constraints on their power. If rulers are not chosen by the people, and if the people cannot change their rulers (other than by extreme means such as violent rebellion), what prevents the rulers from serving their own interests instead of the interests of the community? We don't have to be full-blown Legalists to worry about bad apples in politics. And whatever we think of the arguments against electoral democracy, it is a good means of checking the power of rulers because they can be changed at election time. In imperial China, informal constitutional norms such as censors, court historians, and Confucian educators served to limit the power of the emperor. But emperors could, and sometimes did, ignore informal constitutional norms if it was in their interests to do so.[20] Since the period of reform in the late 1970s, the principle of collective leadership, terms limits, and the introduction of mandatory retirement age has served to limit abuses of power. The constitutional amendment abolishing term limits for the presidency, however, has revived fears of the "bad emperor" problem: how to get rid of a ruler who abuses power without constraints and/or remains in office after becoming physically and mentally disabled. To be fair, collective leadership can still help to restrain, or even overthrow, leaders who become physically or mentally disabled. As a prominent Chinese political analyst put it, the Chinese president may be "first among equals," but he is not "first above equals."[21] Even if collective leadership still serves to constrain the top leader, however, there are serious risks of abuse of power. At this stage, there are different possibilities. The most pessimistic scenario is that the next few years will be characterized first and foremost by increased political repression at home and morally unjustified military adventures abroad. More optimistic scenarios are based on the assumption that somewhat longer terms of rule may be necessary to take on the vested interests that block economic, political, and educational reforms (Franklin Delano Roosevelt, perhaps the most successful U.S. president of the twentieth century, also broke the precedent of two-term limits for the presidency). It would be foolish to make predictions, but one reason for optimism is that the anticorruption drive has succeeded beyond initial expectations, and we can expect more such difficult reforms in the future. The problem, however, is that the Legalist means employed to clamp down on corruption—instilling fear of harsh punishment—has led to negative consequences that may be difficult to remedy.

The main advantage of Legalism is that instilling fear of harsh punishment is an efficient way to swiftly carry out necessary social change. In times of war, few generals would get very far without, say, harsh punishments for deserters. In times of peace, Legalist means may also be necessary to carry out rapid social change. One clear example is the campaign against drunk driving in China. Ten years ago, it would have been almost rude not to serve fiery white liquor to guests in Chinese restaurants.[22] Drunk drivers would head back home, with predictably disastrous consequences. Alarmed by data that showed at least 20 percent of serious road crashes were alcohol related, the Chinese government decided to crack down on drunk driving. Almost overnight, the authorities set up frequent random roadside sobriety checks and rigorously enforced harsh penalties, including compulsory jail time for first offenders and an automatic six-month driving ban. It worked: Attitudes have changed, and drinking and driving is almost universally frowned upon. Death rates caused by drunk drivers have plunged nationwide,[23] and random checks, now few and far between, have become almost superfluous.[24]

The Problem of Corruption

Similar Legalist means were employed to deal with corruption.[25] Before President Xi Jinping assumed power in 2012, paying bribes and showering cadres with lavish meals and gifts were seen as part of ordinary public life. It was difficult to get into good schools and hospitals without greasing the palm of authorities who were supposedly there to safeguard the public good. Promotion to higher-level posts often involved paying bribes to superiors. But corruption reached a tipping point, inflaming public attitudes to the extent of endangering the legitimacy of the political system.[26] In response, the government launched what has turned out to be the longest and most systematic anticorruption campaign in Communist Party history. The various and largely ineffective anticorruption agencies were centralized into one agency: the Central Commission for Discipline Inspection, led by Wang Qishan, and since 2018 the National Supervision Commission, led by Yang Xiaodu. As of 2018, more than one million officials have been netted for corruption, including a dozen high-ranking military officers, several senior executives of state-owned companies, and five national leaders.[27] Cynical observers claim that the whole thing is a means of going after political enemies, but what distinguishes this anticorruption drive from previous ones is that it also *creates* many political enemies, which seems irrational from the point of view of political self-preservation.[28] Whatever the motivation, the effect is clear: The anticorruption drive has worked. Anybody who has dealt with public officials has noticed the changes: Corrupt practices are now almost universally frowned upon, similar to drunk driving. The advantages are obvious: The profits of companies are up because there's no longer any need to pay extras to corrupt public officials.[29] Ordinary citizens perceive the system as less unfair because it's now possible to access public services without paying bribes and gifts to bureaucrats.

The problem is that the anticorruption drive has worked almost too well. It's not just that government officials think twice before engaging in corrupt practices. They think almost all the time about what can go wrong, to the point that decision making has become almost completely paralyzed. Few officials are willing to take risks or consider innovative solutions necessary to solve new and unexpected problems. The procedures for using public funds have become bafflingly complex, and it's safer not to spend any money. It's as though people stop driving cars in response to random checks against drunk drivers on every city block. It's good that bad officials find it harder to misuse public funds, but it's bad that good officials can't use public funds necessary to serve the community. These costs are huge, and growing. China's success over the past three decades is partly explained by the fact that government officials were encouraged to experiment and innovate, thus helping to propel China's reform.[30] But today's conservatism means innovative public officials won't get promoted, and problems won't get fixed. In the long term, paralyzing talented and public-spirited public officials can be deadly.

The second problem related to the anticorruption drive also stems from the fact it has been almost too effective.[31] For each high-level public official who has been brought down by the anticorruption drive, there may be dozens of allies and subordinates who lose prospects of mobility in an ultracompetitive, decades-long race to the apex of political power. These real enemies make the leaders even more paranoid than usual and lead the government to ramp up censorship and curb civil and political rights even more aggressively. So it's not just the political outcasts who feel estranged from the system, but also intellectuals and artists who object to curbs on what they do, as well as businesspeople who worry about political stability and flee abroad with their assets. With yet more social dissatisfaction among elites, leaders further clamp down on real and potential dissent. Knowing their enemies are waiting for the opportunity to pounce,[32] the current leaders are even less likely to give up power (elderly leaders may not worry so much about their own fate because they will soon "visit Karl Marx," but they worry about children and family members). So it's a vicious circle of Legalist means and political repression. Ironically, the most efficient and effective drive to limit abuses of power in recent Chinese history (in the form of the anticorruption campaign) may also have led the leaders of the campaign to remove the most important constraint on their own power (in the form of term and age limits).

What can be done? In retrospect, it may have been a mistake to rely almost exclusively on Legalist means to combat corruption. Legalism can bring short-term political success, but it can also lead to long-term doom, similar to the fate of the Qin dynasty. Chinese history does point to other possibilities, including amnesty for corrupt officials. As the current anticorruption drive was getting under way, reformers argued that general amnesty should be granted to all corrupt officials, with serious policing of the boundaries between private and public, and resources provided to allow them to start afresh.[33] To deal with the problem of *mai guan (买官)* (buying of government posts), public posts could be distributed by lot once officials pass a certain level of qualification, as was done under Emperor Zhu Yijun.[34] But it's too late to start over. What can be done is to wind down the anticorruption drive.[35] Wang Qishan himself said that the anticorruption drive will need to move from an initial deterrent stage to a point where the idea of acting corruptly would not even occur to officials as they went about their business. The next stage can't rely first and foremost on fear of punishment. It must rely on measures that reduce the incentive for corruption, including higher salaries for public officials and more clear separation of economic and political power. It also matters what officials do when nobody is looking: Moral education in the Confucian classics can help to change mindsets in the long term.[36] It's now time to put more trust in public officials and to empower them to do their work on behalf of the public. Any political system must balance the need to constrain government officials from doing bad and empowering them to do good, and the balance in China needs to swing back to the latter. There may be too few constraints on the power of top leaders, but there are too many constraints on the others.[37]

3. Political Meritocracy as the Problem, Political Meritocracy as the Solution

Whatever the constraints on political leaders, however, the meritocratic system won't work well if those leaders tend to come from the same social background. According to the meritocratic ideal, a political system should aim to select and promote leaders with superior ability and virtue. In the Warring States period (475–221 BCE), the market for political talent was basically international. Scholars roamed from state to state hoping to persuade rulers of their superior qualities and to be chosen to serve as ministers and advisors. In principle, the political system should aim to choose the most worthy (and demote the unworthy), regardless of class background. Xunzi expressed this idea: "Promote the worthy and capable without regard to seniority; dismiss the unfit and incapable without hesitation. . . . Although they may be descendants of kings and dukes or scholar-officials and counselors, if they are incapable of devotedly observing the requirements of ritual principles and justice, they should be relegated to the position of commoners. Although they may be descendants of commoners, if they have acquired learning, are upright in conduct, and can adhere to ritual principles, they should be promoted to the post of prime minister, scholar-official, or counselor."[38] Around the same period in a different part of the world, Plato (in *The Republic*) extended meritocratic principles to two other groups. First, the very top ruler(s) should also be chosen according to merit (Xunzi did not extend meritocracy to the position of king). Second, women should also have the opportunity to be rulers. In short, the meritocratic ideal is that everyone should have equal opportunity to serve as a political official regardless of social background, and the political system should aim to choose the most able and virtuous among the contenders.

In reality, however, political hierarchies tend to ossify, and the political selection process often misses out on talent from broad sectors of the population. Eventually the gap between the meritocratic ideal and the frozen reality becomes so large that it threatens the legitimacy of the whole system. In Chinese history, the debates about political meritocracy tend to reappear, with new iterations and interpretations, precisely when the old political hierarchies become ossified, and the governing body could not function well. In the minds of the critics, it is not meritocracy itself that leads to the freeze of political hierarchies.

Quite the reverse, political meritocracy, with new interpretations and practical innovations, is the only solution for improving the political impasse. Historically, the debates about the meritocratic ideal centered around two methods of recommendation and examination, with different emphasis in different times. The most important ways of selecting officials in Chinese history were the recommendation system, the nine-rank system, and the imperial examination system. We will discuss these various methods, in (roughly) chronological order, showing how each innovation occurred in response to the perceived ossification of political hierarchies.[39]

The Recommendation System

The recommendation system made its appearance and was perfected in the Han dynasty (206 BCE–220 CE). At the beginning of the Han, many officials were appointed to participate in political governance because of their meritorious military services, similar to the Legalist-inspired Qin dynasty (221–207 BCE). As the political environment shifted from a turbulent state of war to a period of relative peace, however, the division of work between ministers and generals became clearer and there was a need for more ministers. Therefore, Emperor Han Wu Di (157–87 BCE) further developed the recommendation system, which originated in the period of his father, Han Wendi. Emperor Wu Di named it "以儒取士" (selecting scholars according to the criteria of Confucianism).[40] Officials were selected according to four criteria or "specialties" (四科): virtue and conduct, the study of Confucian classics, a clear understanding of laws and regulations, and a problem-solving mindset.[41]

The rulers of the Han dynasty declared themselves different from the rulers of the Qin dynasty because they aimed to govern the country according to 孝 (filial piety, or reverence for elderly family members). The most important of the four specialties was the first, virtue and conduct, and the most important part of moral conduct was filial piety.[42] As the *History of the Later Han Dynasty* (后汉书) puts it, "Han is a virtue of fire, fire is born from wood, wood promotes fire, so the virtue of fire is filial piety, the image of which in *The Book of Changes* (易经) is Li (礼). . . . Thus the system of Han Dynasty ordered the whole country to learn *The Book of Filial Piety* (孝经), and selected officials by recommendation according to filial piety and a clean record."[43] Such ideas, inspired by *The Book of Changes*, can be seen as metaphysical justifications for the political importance of filial piety in the Han dynasty.

Filial piety gradually became the most important virtue at that time, in both a political and a metaphysical (or religious) sense. As *The Book of Filial Piety* put it: "孝，始于事亲，中于事君，终于立身" [Filial piety, starts with serving parents, unfolds by serving the emperor, and completes itself by establishing oneself in society]. . . . "故当不义，则争之" [When the ones you serve are unjust, argue with them]. . . . "孝悌之至，通于神明，光于四海，无所不通" [When filial piety grows utmost, it could access the spirits and illuminate the four seas—it reaches everywhere].[44] Filial piety was deployed as a critical standard grounded in the moral order of the universe to evaluate the political reality. It demanded serving parents and the emperor by means of upright conduct, in contrast to Legalist-style blind obedience to the status quo. It was also filial to correct the faults of parents and the emperor. That said, the political importance of filial piety can be traced to the social reality at the time. In the Han dynasty, many emperors took over the Court at a very young age, and they needed their mother to help them govern the country. As a consequence, filial piety became an extremely important element to justify obedience to the mothers who acted as *de facto* rulers.[45]

Although filial piety was most important in the Han dynasty, the other three specialties also influenced the selection of scholar-officials. Whereas filial piety relied mainly on recommendations, the other three specialties relied more on examinations. The words 察舉 refer to recommendation by examination. Local officials recommended a certain number of people to the central government every year. The Court gave recommended people suitable official positions, and students at all levels of school underwent some sort of assessment or interview to get political positions.

The original motivation of the recommendation system was to select and promote virtuous and capable candidates for public service, emphasizing the examination of their virtue and capacity rather than 門第 (family status). After the middle of the Eastern Han dynasty (25–220 CE), however, the more powerful families controlled the main power of recommendation, and most of the recommended people came from noble families. The recommendation system lost its initial function of selecting and promoting competent and virtuous officials and degenerated into a way to protect the interests of certain families. Political hierarchies ossified, and rulers ruled for the interests of established elites.

The Nine-Rank System

To solve the problem of ossification, the nine-rank system appeared in the Wei, Jin, Southern, and Northern dynasties (220–589 CE).[46] The court appointed several local recruiters (中正) to recommend talented candidates, and the competent men were ranked by three criteria: family status, moral conduct, and capacity. After ranking they would be appointed to suitable positions. The original intention of setting up the nine-rank system was to correct a series of problems raised by the recommendation system. As *The History of Liu Song Dynasty* (宋书) put it, "The nine-rank system aims to classify the competent men by merit, rather than family status."[47]

At the time of implementation, several noble families dominated the recommendation system, and those from humble families hardly had a chance to be recommended. The most important reform of the nine-rank system was to empower local recruiters (中正), rather than powerful families, with the "right" to recommend public officials. To a certain extent, men from humble families had more opportunities in the new system, compared to the recommendation system. Unfortunately, the new selection system gradually became frozen. In the intellectual history of ancient China, the nine-rank system is often criticized as backward. The most famous criticism was put forward in *The History of the Jin Dynasty* (晋书): "In upper ranks, no one came from the humble families; in lower ones, no one came from the powerful families."[48] Powerful families gradually took charge of the positions of local recruiters, thus entirely controlling the ranking system. Still, it's worth noting the political context of education in the Wei and Jin dynasties. Due to incessant warfare, people were constantly on the run. Official and private schools decayed, and aristocratic families preserved their particular family education by homeschooling or paternal teaching and influence. Hence, the educational situation of aristocratic families often fit their good reputations. But when the official and private schools were revived, the nine-rank system declined and was replaced by the imperial examination system.

The Imperial Examination System

The imperial examination system was founded in the Sui dynasty (581–618) and perfected in the Tang (618–907) and Song dynasties (960–1276). The court selected competent men by imperial examination regardless of family background and without any need for references or recommendations. As a consequence, the monopoly of aristocratic families on the selection of the competent men was almost completely broken, reflecting the spirit of fairness. In the Song dynasty, the imperial examination system was substantially improved. But some Confucian thinkers criticized the scholars' motivation for taking the examinations. If scholars lost their original commitment to rightness and truth, and instead took the exam as a profitable way to gain fame and material interests, those selected as officials would have no virtue at all. Thus they argued for reforming or even abolishing the imperial examination system. For example, Zhu Xi (1130–1200) wrote to the emperor arguing for establishing a separate discipline, called 德行 (virtue and moral conduct), and for abolishing the discipline of 词赋 (composition and rhetoric).[49] The discipline of "virtue and moral conduct" would be different from the other examined disciplines of 经, 子, 史, 时务 (Confucian classics, philosophical writings, history, and current affairs). This new discipline of "virtue and moral conduct" would use recommendations to select virtuous officials and was designed to complement the examined disciplines. Zhu Xi regarded recommendation as a necessary supplement of the imperial examination system and for reminding scholars of the significance of virtue and moral conduct.

Zhu Xi's teachers were even more radical. Cheng Hao (1032–1085) and Cheng Yi (1033–1107), known as "The Two Chengs," were completely against the system of the imperial examinations.[50] They argued that examinations could not test for virtue and were not politically practical.[51] On the one hand, there were too few officials selected by examination, leading to insufficient numbers for the governing body; on the other hand, people selected through examinations would only "博闻强记" ("have encyclopedic knowledge") and would lack the practical ability to deal with politics. Hence they suggested replacing the imperial examination system entirely by recommendation. First, the elders of the counties and the students of the Imperial College would recommend some candidates. Then, the Court would inspect them, assess their abilities as erudite scholars, and appoint them as provisional officials in order to review their political capacities. In the end, the Court would rank scholars through a debate. After all these procedures, the Court would officially appoint every selected scholar to a proper position. Their most innovative suggestion was that the Court could select scholars who prove their political competence through actual political trials. The suggestions of the Two Chengs were not adopted at the time, but they were implemented to a certain extent in later dynasties, and the principle of performance evaluations at lower levels of government still informs political meritocracy in contemporary China.

In short, social critics argued against the recommendation system because it could not give equal opportunities to candidates without powerful family backgrounds and against the examination system because it could not test for virtue or practical political skills. These debates about the problems of actually existing meritocracy took place precisely when political hierarchies became ossified, and there was a need for both new thinking about political meritocracy and new innovations designed to close the gap between the meritocratic ideal and reality. The problem was political meritocracy, and so was the cure.[52]

In fact, contemporary debates about political meritocracy appear against a similar background. For one thing, the gap between rich and poor has exploded during the four decades of economic reform, with the consequence that candidates from wealthy and politically powerful families have unfair advantages in the meritocratic competition for political power. The fact that almost all top leaders are men further exposes the gap between the ideal and the reality of political meritocracy. And the corruption problem threatens to undermine the moral legitimacy of the public officials who do make it through the system. Similar to imperial times, social critics and political reformers in China argue that the solution is not to abandon the ideal of political meritocracy, but rather to propose innovations designed to reduce the gap between the ideal of meritocracy and the reality.[53] What's different this time, however, is that political meritocracy, even in ideal form, is not sufficient to legitimatize the whole political system. The value of democracy is widely advocated by both the Chinese government and its critics, and nobody argues for establishing a purely meritocratic political community today. It would be hard to persuade people that they should be totally excluded from political power. Plato himself recognized (in *The Republic*) the need to propagate a "Noble Lie" that the guardians deserve absolute power because they have gold in their souls, unlike everybody else. Regimes like North Korea can propagate such myths about the quasi-divine status of their rulers because they are closed to the rest of the world, but no modern open society can get away with it. In short, it's hard to imagine a modern government today that can be seen as legitimate in the eyes of the people without any form of democracy. So the question is how to inject an element of democracy into the political system. In a Chinese context, the special challenge is how to legitimize a hierarchical political system informed by the principle of political meritocracy to the majority of people who are formally excluded from political power. With 90 million members, the Chinese Communist Party is the world's second-largest political party, but it's still composed of a small fraction of the 1.4 billion people.

4. Justifying a Hierarchical Political System to Those outside the System

The key justification for political rule is that rulers serve the people. But who decides if the people are being served? In the Confucian tradition, contrary to popular perception, the people have an important role. As Joseph Chan explains, "Confucians are not interested in authority merely as an institution justified externally by certain objective reasons such as the promotion of people's well-being. Authority is also a kind of *relationship* or *bond* between the ruler and the ruled (or in contemporary terms, between those who govern and the governed). What makes the relationship truly authoritative is not just the ruler's ability to protect and promote the people's well-being, but the willing acceptance of his rule by the people."[54] Confucius himself asserted the importance of winning the hearts of the people (20.1), and gaining the willing compliance of the people is a recurring theme in the Confucian tradition. The Song dynasty thinker and politician Su Dongpo (1037–1101) spells out the flip side in his counsel to Emperor Shenzong: "He who is able to command the support of the millions becomes a king, while he who alienates their support becomes a solitary private individual (独夫). The basis of the ruler's authority (人主) lies, therefore, entirely in the support of the people in their hearts. . . . And when an emperor loses the support of the people, it spells his ruin."[55] In short, the legitimacy of political rule is based both on the (objective) idea that the ruler promotes the well-being of the people and the (subjective) idea that the people willingly accept the ruler's authority. Without the compliance of the people, the ruler's rule, and the whole political system, is under threat of collapse. But how can we know that the people accept the ruler's authority? The answer in modern-day electoral democracies, of course, is that winning the people's support by means of free and fair competitive elections is the way to measure willing acceptance by the people. As argued above (section 1), however, competitive elections at the top would wreck the advantages of the meritocratic system. And whatever we think of the normative arguments for and against elections, we can safely assume that the Chinese political system is not about the selection of its top rulers by means of free and fair competitive elections in the foreseeable future.

So we are back to the question of how to secure the people's endorsement of a hierarchical political system without democratic elections. In the case of China, the Chinese Communist Party has drawn on three sources of legitimacy: nationalism, performance legitimacy, and political meritocracy.[56] Although all three sources of legitimacy have been important at different times to a certain extent, perhaps the strongest source of legitimacy in the reform era has been performance legitimacy in the form of economic growth. Over the past four decades, there has been a widespread consensus that the government should strive for high growth rates because growth was seen as key to poverty reduction. Hence, government officials could be promoted based on economic performance above all else without much controversy.

Today, however, the problems are much more diverse, some directly attributable to the lopsided emphasis on economic growth: rampant pollution, a huge gap between rich and poor, precarious social welfare, and an explosion of government debt, not to mention massive corruption. In the future, the government will lose support if it doesn't deal with those problems, whatever the rate of economic growth. Here things become more complicated for a political system that prides itself on meritocratic mechanisms for the selection and promotion of leaders. Should government officials be assessed according to their ability to deliver economic growth, to improve social welfare, to reduce corruption, to protect the environment, to reduce the gap between rich and poor, to reduce government debt, or to achieve some combination of these goals? It is impossible to resolve these issues in a noncontroversial way, and there are bound to be many winners and losers no matter the decision. Hence, the government needs more input from the people, not just to help decide on priorities, but also to take the heat off when large constituencies are unhappy with some policies. More generally, as China modernizes, there will be more demands for political participation by the people.[57]

In short, democracy is necessary to save political meritocracy in China. Legalist-style repression can work in the short term, but there must be more deliberation and participation in the long term. This is not to deny that the Chinese political system already incorporates strong elements of democracy. Over nine hundred million farmers have participated in village-level elections since 1988.[58] Cadres are selected through a three-ticket system that includes democratic evaluation and the election of the party's Standing Committee in addition to meritocratic methods such as examinations. He Baogang argues that public deliberation is increasingly becoming an indispensable element in decision-making processes.[59] There is already a degree of consultation in the political system—for example, it took five years for the Property Law to pass the National People's Congress following almost endless rounds of expert advice and public debate.[60] But all these democratic practices are not sufficient: More citizens will need to argue about what works in a wide range of domains and to have a greater say. Such openness is necessary not just to improve decision making but also to diffuse the sense of responsibility for those decisions. This will entail more freedom of speech and association and more mechanisms for consultation and deliberation within and outside the party, as well as transparent mechanisms to remove public officials who perform badly. All the innovations of modern democratic societies, such as sortition, open public hearings, deliberative polling, and referenda on key issues, could help to stabilize the political system. And more firmly establishing the rule of law is necessary to protect basic human rights.[61]

Even with more participation and deliberation at lower levels of government, however, it will be a challenge to legitimize the political system to those outside the power structure, especially to citizens who seek to make a positive difference in Chinese society without going through the official selection and promotion process for political leaders. Competitive elections at the top can give all citizens the hope (or illusion) that they can participate in political power, but this option is not open to a political system informed by the ideal of political meritocracy.[62] So what can be done to expand political opportunities to the vast majority of citizens? The Confucian tradition, it should be recognized, may not have much to offer in this respect. As Zhang Yongle argues, Confucian education emphasized virtue "in order to maintain a sense among the people that the career of a politician requires special talents and training, and perhaps only suits a minority of people."[63] However, there is also a need to affirm the idea that "the average person can also participate in public affairs at the grassroots level, and even realize outstanding achievements and achieve recognition by the state." Zhang argues that the Maoist tradition offers political insights. China's revolution, inspired by Mao's thought, allowed for the possibility that average people could achieve recognition by the state. For one thing, there was a less intellectual view of what constitutes political merit: "those who were selected as model workers often were able to use the opportunity to enter the political stage, which helped to forge the common belief that ordinary jobs can offer valuable contributions to society and even the possibility of being rewarded with a leadership position."[64] In Mao's time, however, valuing workers was accompanied by a radical form of anti-intellectualism. Today, the challenge is to value different forms of political merit without radical critiques of forms that fall outside those valued by the state (and without violence directed at people from "bad" class backgrounds).

The greatest resource for maintaining legitimacy, Zhang argues, is the "mass line," which stems from the revolutionary era:

The mass line, the Party term for a policy aimed at cultivating contacts with the common people, emphasized the idea of coming from the masses and going among the masses. It represents opposition to the idea that a minority or elites should be able to pursue top-down policies. Instead it argues that the understanding of truth is a process that is constantly being revised by collective practice and that close contact with the masses is necessary to reach a more realistic understanding of the country's situation, which in turn is critical for formulating the correct party line and policies. . . . To put the concept of mass line into practice, it's necessary to "find the masses." This not only requires cadres to go out into the masses, but also necessitates a certain level of organization on the part of grassroots society, in order to create connections between the grassroots, policymakers, and the executive branch of government. With these connections, policymakers can hear the voice of ordinary people and improve the responsiveness of their policies, which helps policymakers.[65]

Zhang's argument is thought provoking. The mass line put into practice is a way of securing widespread legitimacy for the political system without a system of competitive elections. Today, it is encouraging that up-and-coming public officials in China typically need to spend extended periods in poor rural regions to help to sensitize cadres to the needs of the worst-off members of the community.[66] That said, there may be a need to further democratize the mass line. Similar to the political practice in the Ming and Qing dynasties, sortition can be used as a method to distribute cadres to local communities, which can also minimize corruption and favoritism. There is also a need to increase opportunities for self-organization at the grassroots level.

Perhaps the deepest problem with the Confucian tradition, however, is the assumption that the best form of life involves serving the political community. In societies with a Confucian heritage, it seems likely that political leaders will continue to have the highest social status and those without political power may not feel a sense of (equal) social worth. So there is a need to affirm the social value of "nonpolitical" ways of life.[67] Here we can turn to the Daoist critique of political meritocracy in the pre-Qin period for inspiration.[68] Laozi, the originator of Daoist thought, bluntly put forward the idea of not valuing or employing the virtuous: "Not to value and employ men of superior ability is the way to keep the people from rivalry among themselves; not to prize articles which are difficult to procure is the way to keep them from becoming thieves; not to show them what is likely to excite their desires is the way to keep them minds from disorder."[69] The basic idea is that any sort of competitive society—including a society that encourages competition according to a conception of political merit—will make people, especially the "losers," envious and miserable, so it's best to discourage any form of competition and desire for a better life. Hence, "the sage, in the exercise of government . . . constantly tries to keep people without knowledge and without desire, and where there are those who have knowledge, to keep them from presuming to act on it."[70] The ruler should limit politics driven by competitive feelings and ambition, which means not employing the wise and the virtuous.

In the same vein, Zhuangzi discouraged use of the wise and virtuous. He shares Laozi's view that "elevating the worthy" will lead to a competitive and chaotic society: "if you raise the men of talent to office, you will create disorder; making the people strive with one another for promotion; if you employ men for their wisdom, the people will rob each other." Zhuangzi goes further by casting doubt on the whole idea of distinguishing between those with more worth and less. Everybody has limited talent and biased perspectives: "no one has covered or extended the whole range of truth . . . there is a limit to our life, but to knowledge there is no limit. With what is limited to pursue after what is unlimited is a perilous thing; and when, knowing this, we still seek the increase of our knowledge, the peril cannot be averted." Humans can only dwell in specific places, occupy a specific situation, obtain limited knowledge, yet they often take their own view as the whole truth and argue endlessly from and for their limited perspective: "So it is that we have the contentions between the Confucians and the Mohists, the one side affirming what the other denies and vice versa." And however brilliant a sage may be, he cannot avoid becoming entangled in social connections and political plots that lead to disaster: "Long Feng was beheaded; Bi Gan had his heart torn out; Chang Hong was ripped open; and Zi Xu was reduced to pulp. Worthy as these four men were, they did not escape dreadful deaths." So the solution is to abandon the whole idea of pursing wisdom: "in the age of perfect virtue, they attached no value to wisdom, nor employed men of ability."[71]

The Lao-Zhuang tradition may seem extreme in its anti-intellectualism. But it does remind us of our necessarily limited perspectives and of the need to distrust those who arrogantly claim access to the whole truth and confidently assert their political effectiveness. The solution is not to abandon the idea that some perspectives are better than others—even Zhuangzi would agree that those who are aware of their limitations are better than those who aren't. Nor is the solution to abandon the political aim of selecting and promoting those with above average talent and virtue. What must be done is to employ officials with diverse talents and different perspectives to help correct for the necessary limitations of any one person's perspective. Cao Feng shows how the Huang-Lao tradition drew on Daoist insights for political purposes: "Since it was a political ideology, Huang-Lao thought had to use people of talent and virtue to be carried out, and therefore could not reject the talented and virtuous as the Lao-Zhuang tradition did, let alone consider them to be initiators of turmoil. On the contrary, why sages were needed, what kind of sages were needed, and how to make use of them were important elements of Huang-Lao political thought."[72] The Huang-Lao tradition emphasized that the monarch needs to recognize he cannot do everything on his own and hence needs to employ public officials with superior talents. Even the wisest of the sages has limited knowledge and perspectives and needs supplementary assistance (and criticism): "since the ruler's wisdom and talents are not sufficient to spread his splendor across lands and seas, he is surrounded by high ministers who assist him." To allow for public officials to flourish and make contributions, the monarch must practice inaction: "if the ruler is able to renounce his own wisdom, talent, and accomplishments, he will be able to bring fully into play his people's wisdom, talent, and accomplishments." Given necessarily limited knowledge and perspectives, the monarch should strive to employ different kinds of public officials with different backgrounds and different skills: diverse "types of men have opposite characters, however sages can still use them in a tolerant way. . . . If guarding just one corner means leaving out the rest of the world, and selecting one species means giving up all other beings, one is sure to achieve very little: the reach of one's administration will certainly be very narrow."[73] In short, the monarch should be aware of his limitations and make comprehensive use of public officials with diverse backgrounds and talents.

In a political system led by a monarch, the Huang-Lao school of thought might counsel against a cult of personality that portrays him as all-wise and benevolent. Other things being equal, a system of collective leadership is best to ensure that diverse perspectives can inform the policy-making process at the very top. In a large country such as China, collective leadership at the top would also need to be supported by an extensive bureaucracy at different levels of government staffed with a wide range of public officials from diverse backgrounds with diverse talents. But even this kind of system would not fully alleviate Daoist worries about the downside of political meritocracy: In the modern world, even a well-functioning political meritocracy that selects and promotes public officials with diverse talents and backgrounds would need to be supported by an ultracompetitive educational system that aims to identify and educate those with above-average ability and talent, and the dominant competitive ethos of that society will lead to endless striving for success that causes misery for the "losers" and hence sows the seeds of social disorder. These Daoist worries would be further exacerbated in a capitalist economic system that rewards entrepreneurs and companies who successfully invent new needs and desires for consumers who are never supposed to be satisfied with the status quo.

So what can be done to soften the deleterious societal effects of political meritocracy in the modern age?[74] Perhaps the best way is to emphasize that the role of the professional public official is not the only way to lead a meaningful life. This means attributing more social (and material) value for "non-political" ways of life that contribute to the social good, such as the work of farmers, family caretakers, and manual workers. It also means allowing for mechanisms that cast doubt on the whole meritocratic system, but without really threatening the whole system. Perhaps the most fascinating social development in contemporary China has been the rapid spread of what we can term a "culture of cuteness": a public affirmation of cute animals, robots, and emojis that inform everyday social interaction. The trend started in Japan in the 1970s[75]—when Japan was largely ruled by a meritocratically selected bureaucracy selected from an ultracompetitive educational system. It was led by teenage girls and eventually spread to other sectors of society. Over the past decade or so, the culture of cuteness has spread to China almost like wildfire. The streets of Chinese cities are populated with ridiculously cute dogs and cats,[76] and the use of cute emojis is the norm for communication on social media, even in official settings such as exchanges between university administrators.[77]

It's worth asking why the culture of cuteness has planted social roots so quickly and so deeply in China. One explanation is

FIGURE 2. Cute dog in Shanghai with counter-revolutionary clothing.
Photograph by Wang Pei.

that it's helpful for meritocratic competition: Viewing cute im-
ages promotes careful behavior and narrows attentional focus,
with potential benefits for learning and office work.[78] But the
deeper reason may be both disturbing and encouraging for defenders of political meritocracy. On the one hand, the culture of
cuteness represents a kind of rebellion against the whole system:
Instead of affirming the value of boring and hard-working (largely
male) bureaucrats who serve the public good, it affirms the value
of playful and somewhat self-indulgent ways of life. As Simon
May puts it, the culture of cuteness articulates "a nascent will to
repudiate the ordering of human relations by power, or at least
to question our assumptions about who has power and to what
end. This is a will that Cute can vividly convey precisely because
it usually involves a relationship to a vulnerable object or to an

object that flaunts, or flirts with, vulnerability. It is a will to liberation from the power paradigm that many, especially in the West and Japan, but perhaps ordinary Chinese people too, might be expected to affirm as an antidote to a century and more of unparalleled brutality."[79] On the other hand, the culture of cuteness reduces the desire to join the race to the top, which helps to placate the "losers" in the political meritocracy and hence stabilizes the meritocratic system.[80]

To summarize, if the task is to legitimize hierarchical political meritocracy in a modern society that values equal social worth and participation in politics by ordinary people, we can learn much not just from Confucians and liberal democrats, but also from Maoists and Daoists. More specifically, both Maoist and Daoist ideas can help to legitimize the system among those left out from the official power hierarchies in political meritocracies without the safety valve of electoral competition for higher-level political posts. The Maoist mass line can help to provide avenues for grassroots participation in politics and make elites more responsive to the needs of the masses. And Daoist-style skepticism about the desirability of the whole meritocratic system can help to legitimatize alternative avenues for socially valued ways of life such as the culture of cuteness that gives meaning to the lives of those left out of the political hierarchies.

At the end of the day, however, we are left with several ironies. Confucians argue that the best life involves service to the political community, but the only way to justify Confucian-inspired political hierarchy today is to organize a political system that doesn't value serving the public as the highest form of life. There may also be trade-offs between the different ways of addressing the main challenges of political meritocracy. Strong, Legalist-style measures to deal with corruption may be most effective in the short term, but they can further ossify political hierarchies (because innovation is discouraged and officials become cautious and conservative) and lead to an even more closed society (because leaders worry about backlash from their growing list of enemies). In the long term, a judicious mixture of Confucian-style soft power combined with democratic openness, Maoist-style mass line, and Daoist-style skepticism about the whole political system will help to reinvigorate political meritocracy in China. What won't change, however, is the need to identify and select public officials with above-average ability and a willingness to serve the political community over and above their own private and family interests. That ideal goes back over two millennia in China, and it will continue to inform the political system in the foreseeable future.

Even if China succeeds in closing the gap between the ideal and practice of political meritocracy, however, it doesn't follow that Chinese rulers should try to export this political ideal abroad. For one thing, the ideal might be difficult or impossible to implement in a political culture that lacks a history of complex bureaucratic rule with argumentation about the ideal of political meritocracy. Nor do we mean to imply that political meritocracy is the only morally justified way of securing the hierarchical relation between rulers and the ruled. And when it comes to international relations, different kinds of principles should inform relations between states, as we will see in the next chapter.

3

Just Hierarchy between States

ON THE NEED FOR RECIPROCITY

A humane authority would keep in good order the obligations
between small and large countries, between the strong and the
weak, and would rigorously maintain them. The important
points of ritual would be observed with the extreme of good
form.

—*XUNZI*, 10.20

A MORALLY JUSTIFIED hierarchy within a state, as we saw,
involves a conception of service: The rulers are supposed to serve
the people. The rulers needn't be pure altruists, but the state's
policies should aim mainly to benefit the people rather than the
rulers, and such policies are more likely if the rulers are at least
partly motivated by the desire to serve the people. Morally justified hierarchies between states are different. The rulers of states
owe their first obligations to their own people, and they cannot
be expected to systematically sacrifice the interests of their own
people for the interests of people in other states. Hierarchical relations between states must be reciprocal: They must benefit

people in both powerful and weaker states. In other words, they must be "win-win."

But there are two kinds of reciprocity. One kind—let's call it "weak reciprocity"—is the ideal that hierarchical relations between states should be mutually advantageous. Each state thinks from the perspective of its own state (more precisely, the rulers think of the interests of their own people), and they strike deals or make alliances if they are beneficial to (the people of) both states. But weak reciprocity is fragile. Once the situation changes and the deal is no longer advantageous to one of the states, that state can simply opt out of the deal, just as the Trump administration seems to have decided to renegotiate or scrap free trade accords (and even security alliances) on the grounds that those deals no longer benefit the United States (if they ever did). Weaker states are particularly vulnerable under the terms of weak reciprocity because they are subject to the whims of the stronger states that can decide to change the terms of the deal. Another kind of reciprocity—let's call it "strong reciprocity"—is the ideal that both states come to think of their alliances from the perspective of both states, no longer simply from the perspective of their own state. The rulers no longer think simply in terms of benefiting their own people, and they are willing to stick with deals or alliances even if (temporarily?) the deals may be more beneficial to the people of other states. Moreover, what counts as the interest of each state itself comes to be influenced, at least partly, by the interests (and culture and history) of the other state: There is mutual learning that affects how people think of their own interests and conceptions of the good life. A former enemy state can come to be seen as a friendly state with shared interests and values. One example might be the relations between the United Kingdom and the United States. Strong reciprocity is more demanding (and perhaps more rare) than weak reciprocity, but it is more stable and beneficial for the weaker states.

Does the ideal of reciprocity, whether strong or weak, between hierarchical states still matter in the modern world? Not on the (juridical) face of it. We are supposed to live in an age of equal sovereign states. The Peace of Westphalia treaty in 1648 set in stone the ideal of equality between sovereign states who are supposed to respect each other's sovereignty and refrain from interfering in each other's domestic affairs. This ideal originated in Europe and slowly spread to the rest of the world. In 1945, the United Nations generalized the one person one vote principle to the level of states, with each state given equal representation regardless of size or wealth. Much theorizing in (Western) international relations is based on this ideal of formal and juridical equality between sovereign states.

In reality, however, states are neither equal nor sovereign. As David A. Lake puts it, "sovereignty is a bundle of rights or authorities that can be divided among different levels of governance and different rulers. . . . Treating sovereignty as divisible allows authority between states to vary along continua of lesser or greater hierarchy."[1] It takes only a moment's reflection to realize that the global order consists of a hierarchy between different states, with some states having more *de facto* power than others. Nobody really cares about the fact that Nicaragua didn't sign on to the Paris Climate Accord, but President Trump's decision to withdraw from this accord may be a global disaster because of the United States' disproportionate power to set the global agenda. Even the United Nations expresses the fact of global hierarchy: The most important decisions are often made at the level of the Security Council, which distinguishes between permanent members, nonpermanent members of the Security Council, and ordinary member states. That's why rising powers such as India and Brazil fight hard (thus far unsuccessfully) for recognition as permanent members on the Security Council.

If theorists of international relations aim to develop theories that explain the behavior of states and (more ambitiously) predict outcomes in the international system, then theorizing should be more attentive to the reality of hierarchy between states. There may also be good normative reasons to justify hierarchies between states. If it's just a matter of strong states bullying weaker ones to get what they want, normative theorists can just step aside. But strong states do good things for the global order as a whole. However much we worry about "rogue" leaders in strong states that sabotage global agreements, it would be much harder to forge agreements for dealing with global challenges such as climate change in an international system characterized by states with equal power to shape and withdraw from global accords.[2] Hierarchical systems can also contribute to international peace: As Yan Xuetong puts it, "if we examine recent international history, we can see that in those areas that implemented hierarchical norms, international peace was better maintained than it was in areas that had norms for equality. During the Cold War, the equal status of the United States and the Soviet Union was such that they undertook many proxy wars in order to compete for hegemony, while their special status in NATO and the Warsaw Pact, respectively, enabled them to prevent the members of those alliances from engaging in military conflict with one another."[3] Moreover, hierarchical arrangements can actually benefit weaker states because this sense of dominance means that states have extra responsibilities. Security hierarchies, for example, reduce the level of defense expenditure in subordinate states.[4] Unequal economic power can also benefit weaker states. Rather than insisting on equal reciprocity with weaker states, strong states can gain their support by allowing differential international norms that work in their favor: For example "in the cooperation of the 10+1—the Association of Southeast Asian Nations (ASEAN) and China—China is required to implement the norm of zero tariffs in agricultural trade before the ASEAN states do. This unequal norm enabled the economic cooperation of the 10+1 to develop more rapidly than that between Japan and ASEAN. Japan's demand for equal tariffs with ASEAN slowed the progress of economic cooperation with the ASEAN states, which lags far behind that of China and ASEAN."[5] With extra powers come extra responsibilities, and it's not completely utopian to suggest that strong states do occasionally act on those responsibilities and should be held accountable if they fail to do so. At the very least, we need theories that can help us distinguish between good and bad forms of international hierarchies and help us think of how to promote the good forms and avoid the bad ones. Hence, as Lane puts it, "like a Gestalt shift picture . . . refocusing on hierarchy reveals an alternative reality that has always been with us if we would but choose to see it."[6]

But we don't need a Gestalt shift as much as a return to ancient ways of thinking. In both classical India and classical China, political thinkers developed rich and diverse theories of international politics that took hierarchy between states for granted. We can mine these ancient theories for contemporary insights. Some political thinkers in ancient India and China defended the ideal of weak reciprocity between hierarchical states, and others argued for strong reciprocity. This chapter leads off with a discussion of (some) ancient Indian views of hierarchical global order, followed by a discussion of (some) ancient Chinese views of hierarchical global order. The final section will argue for an ideal of "one world, two hierarchical systems" that may be appropriate for future forms of global order.

1. Hierarchical Ideals of Global Order in Ancient India

In ancient India, the most systematic work in interstate relations is Kautilya's *Arthasastra*: The English translation runs over 800 pages, more than half of which are devoted to foreign policy and war.[7] Kautilya probably flourished in the first century CE, and tradition identified him as the shrewd minister who brought the king to power and established the Maurya dynasty. He makes Machiavelli look like a sentimental idealist; had his work been more influential in Europe, we'd be using the term "Kautilyan" rather than "Machiavellian" to describe amoral realism in international politics. Writing in a time of small kingdoms ruled by monarchs, he assumed a state of warfare as the norm. The ruler should do his best to expand his territory, without moral or religious constraints. More than that, he should go out of his way to prey on people's superstitious beliefs to further his own ends. Consider the following list of tactics for assassinating the enemy:

> During a pilgrimage for worshipping a divinity, there are numerous places that (the enemy) will visit to pay homage according to his devotion. At those places, he should employ trickery on him. Upon him, as he enters a temple, he should make a false wall or a stone fall by releasing a mechanical device; or set off a shower of stones or weapons from an upper chamber; or let a door panel plunge; or release a door bar attached to a wall and secured at one end. Or, he should make the statue, banner, or weapons of the god fall upon him. Or, in places where he stands, sits, or walks, he should arrange for poison to be used against him by means of the cow dung that is smeared, the scented water that is sprinkled, or the flowers and powders that are offered. Or, he should waft over to him

lethal smoke concealed by perfume. Or, by releasing a pin, he should make him plunge into a well with spikes or a pitfall that is located beneath his bed or seat and whose top surface is held together by a mechanical device.[8]

Kautilya's most important contribution to interstate political thinking is the theory of *mandala*, the circle of kingdoms. As Patrick Olivelle explains, "A king is surrounded in a circle by other states, and because they have common boundaries with him, they are his natural enemies. Around these enemy kingdoms is a second circle of kingdoms. Because they abut the territories of enemy kings of the first circle, they become his natural allies: my enemy's enemy is my friend. Those forming the third outer circle would, by the same logic, be the enemies of his allies, and thus his own enemies—and so on."[9] The theory of *mandala* assumes rough parity between states in the sense that all states can wage wars against one another, but, to repeat, there is no "modern" proviso about the need to respect the territorial integrity of states, hence no theorizing that assumes equality of states. Quite the opposite, the constant quest for expansion of territory means that the size, wealth, and power of states shift in accordance with the gains and losses of territory that result from a near-constant state of warfare.

But the principle that the enemy of my enemy is my friend can also lead to mutually beneficial outcomes: To help justify the CCP's alliance with the Kuomintang of China (KMT) in the struggle against Japanese imperialism, Mao Zedong famously said, "[w]e should support whatever our enemies oppose and oppose whatever our enemies support."[10] This principle also helped to justify *rapprochement* with the United States when both countries had the Soviet Union as a common enemy. Kautilya himself affirms that kings should strive for mutually beneficial peace pacts: "when the gain is equal, one should conclude a peace pact."[11] Even weaker kings can initiate peace pacts with stronger powers: "When a weaker king is overwhelmed by a stronger king with a superb army, he should quickly submit with a peace pact by offering his treasury, his army, himself, or his land."[12] But "weak reciprocity" in the form of a mutually beneficial peace pact is temporary at best. For one thing, a peace pact cannot fundamentally challenge the ally/enemy configuration specified by the theory of the *mandala*. A peace pact formed by two natural enemies with contiguous boundaries is possible but deeply unstable. And boundaries can change, so that one's natural ally can become a natural enemy if conquests result in two formerly friendly states with contiguous boundaries. More fundamentally, a ruler can—and should— disregard the peace pact when it's no longer in his interest to maintain it. Kautilya takes this point to its profoundly cynical extreme: "When he wishes to outwit an enemy who is corrupt, hasty, disrespectful, and lazy or who is ignorant, he should tell him, 'We have entered into a peace pact' without fixing the region, time, or task. Through the confidence generated by the peace pact, he should find his vulnerable points and attack him."[13] Hence, a Kautilyan-style "peace pact" should be viewed as nothing more than a strategy designed "to outsmart, outmaneuver, and finally overpower the king with whom he has concluded the pact."[14] Rulers should never lose sight that the ultimate aim is territorial conquest: Bigger is better, and too bad for the smaller states that end up on the losing side. Some states become so large that they are outside the *mandala* theory of ally and enemy: Large states led by powerful kings can be neutral. And what happens when a powerful "neutral" king conquers much of the (known) world? At that point, is it possible to move from "weak reciprocity" to a more stable "strong reciprocity" between hierarchical states? Kaultilya does speak of the "righteous king" as a protector of social harmony,[15] but it's Ashoka who shows the way.

Ashoka Maurya, commonly known as Ashoka and also as Ashoka the Great, was a successful conqueror who ended up ruling almost all of the Indian subcontinent from circa 268 BCE to 232 BCE. He relied on Kautilyan-style methods to conquer territories, including the brutal war against the Kalingas (today's Orissa) with approximately 100,000 killed and 150,000 taken away as captives. At the height of his power, however, Ashoka had a conversion to Buddhism that radically changed his outlook from warmongering to peace-loving (his experience is perhaps the most striking counterexample to the dictum that power corrupts). He expressed profound regret for the Kalinga war and propounded a commitment to *dharma*, which can be roughly translated as the moral way, in Rock Edicts throughout his empire. But this commitment to spreading morality was not restricted to his own empire: "In the imperial territories among the Greeks and Kambojas, Nabhakas and Nabhapanktis, Bhojas and Pitinikas, Andras and Parindas, everywhere people follow the Beloved of the Gods' instruction in *Dhamma* [aka *Dharma*]. Even where the envoys of the Beloved of the Gods have not gone, people hear of his conduct according to *Dhamma*, his precepts and his instructions in *Dhamma*, and they follow *Dhamma* and will continue to follow it. What is obtained by this is victory everywhere, and everywhere victory is pleasant. This pleasure has been obtained through victory by *Dhamma*."[16] This vision seemed to express an ideal rather than a reality, but Ashoka sent his "envoys of the Beloved of the Gods" to faraway lands to spread the moral way.

What is the content of the moral way? At minimum, it means a commitment to peace and nonviolence. The commitment to life, Buddhist-style, extends to all forms of life, not just human

and society. In fact, he begins with the assumption that
n nature tends toward badness" (23.1). If people follow
dily natures and indulge their natural inclinations, aggres-
ss and exploitation are sure to develop, resulting in cruel
y and poverty (19.1). Fortunately, that's not the end of the
Human beings can be "made good by conscious exertion"
They can learn to contain their natural desires and enjoy
nefits of peaceful and cooperative social existence.

Xunzi on Hierarchical Rituals[23]

ey to transformation is ritual (23.3).[24] By learning and par-
ting in rituals, people can learn to contain their desires,
will be a fit between people's actual desires and the good
ble in society, and social peace and material well-being will
(19.1). Rituals provide bonds not based solely on kinship
llow people to partake of the benefits of social existence.
hat exactly is ritual? Xunzi's account of ritual contains fea-
that are familiar to contemporary accounts of ritual: It is
al practice (as opposed to behavior involving only one per-
it is grounded in tradition (as opposed to newly invented
practices), it is noncoercive (in contrast to legal punish-
s), and the details can be changed according to the social
ext.
t Xunzi's account of rituals is driven by normative consid-
ns, and he highlights two considerations that may be less
iar to readers today. In English, the term "ritual" tends to
ote paying behavioral lip service to social norms. The word
al" is often preceded by "empty," meaning that it's devoid of
emotions. But that's not ritual in Xunzi's sense: Ritual must
ve emotion and behavior. As Xunzi puts it, "Rituals reach
highest perfection when both emotion and form are fully

beings: "I have enforced the law against killing certain animals and many others, but the greatest progress of righteousness among men comes from the exhortation in favor of non-injury to life and abstention from killing living beings."[17] It includes the provision of medical knowledge to foreign countries, prompting Patrick Olivelle to comment that "the intention of Ashoka in sending these missions is very clear: it was a missionary effort to spread his dharma philosophy, to get rulers of these countries to adopt Ashoka's moral philosophy in their internal administration and external affairs. . . . This is very similar to the way Christian missionaries acted in countries they were attempting to evangelize."[18]

But Ashoka's moral way refers to the idea of building a common morality that draws on different moralities while respecting difference. In that sense, his "envoys of the Beloved of the Gods" were not like Christian missionaries who tried to spread what they considered to be the truth and (implicitly or explicitly) downgraded other moral systems. Consider what Ashoka said about intercommunal relations. Ashoka's aim was not just peaceful co-existence among deeply divided communities: he also aimed for mutual learning which requires restrained and respectful speech on the part of the "Beloved of the gods":

There should not be honor of one's own sect and condemnation of others' sect without any common ground. Such slighting should be for specified grounds only. On the other hand, the sects of others should be honored for this ground or that. Thus doing, one helps his own sect to grow and benefits the sects of others, too. Doing otherwise, one hurts his own sect and injures the sects of others. For whosoever honors his own sect and condemns the sects of others wholly from devotion to his own sect, i.e., the thought "How I may glorify my own sect" and acting thus injures more gravely his own sect on the contrary. Hence concord alone is commendable, in this sense all should listen and be willing to listen to the doctrines professed by others, this is, in fact, the desire of His Sacred Majesty.[19]

If envoys refrain from excessive self-glorification and immoderate criticism of the other sects, they can maintain the peace and avoid humiliating other sects. But they must also strive to transform their own views: As Rajeev Bhargava explains, "Ashoka says that those seeking improvement in their ethical views should not only communicate with others with different perspectives in order to learn from them but even follow their precepts, 'obey' them. Thinking as if you were in someone else's shoes may not on occasions be sufficient; you have to act with their shoes on. This practical ethical engagement brings an experiential dimension that could be ethically transformative."[20] Clearly the aim is close to what we termed "strong reciprocity": Both sides respect each other's differences while attempting to learn from each other and forge a common morality that draws on the morality of both sides. There may be unequal power relations and hierarchies between states—Ashoka sends envoys to less powerful states, not the other way around—but we are a long way from Christian missionaries who aim to spread the Gospel to morally backward natives. In today's world, what most grates intellectuals in post-colonial countries are moralizing sermons by modern-day envoys—hectoring politicians, crusading journalists, nongovernmental organization (NGO) activists, culturally insensitive tourists, not to mention card-carrying religious missionaries—from Western countries with a dark track record of racism, colonialism, and imperialism. Surely relations between unequal powers could be improved if representatives from

great powers exercised Ashokan-styl speech in dealing with weaker countr possibility of genuine (economic or s est between states, but such conflicts modern-day states adhered to Asho may be dead, but let his ideals live or

It could be argued that Ashoka pu respectful and restrained speech prim mestic policy, that is, for the sake of p communal relations in his own empire lieved in the universality of his Budd they also provide useful guidelines for out, his ideals resonate with ideals of st countries put forward by political thin well. Let us now turn to proposals for chies that were developed by Xunzi, pe rist of international relations in ancient see, proposed a mechanism—ritual—th strong reciprocity between hierarchical

2. Hierarchical Ideals of G
in Ancient Chin

As in ancient India, ancient Chinese thi the idea of hierarchy in social life. Xunzi (explicitly extolled the virtues of hierarchy as one of the three founding fathers of Cor Confucius and Mencius). He has been tain posed influence on the Legalists—the I China[22]—but his ideas had great influen tics of East Asian societies. His writings ar and he deliberately avoids utopian assum

realized" (19.7). The main point of ritual is to civilize our animal natures, and if people are just going through the outward routines without any emotion, they are not likely to transform their natures. The ritual needs to involve, or trigger, an emotional response, so that it will have an effect on the participants during the ritual and beyond the ritual itself. Hence, rituals often need to be accompanied by music that helps to trigger those emotional responses (Xunzi devoted a whole chapter on the moral and political effects of music). Still today, in Chinese the word "ritual" is often followed by the word for "music" (礼乐), as though the two ideas are almost inseparable.

Second, and equally important, Xunzi's account of ritual involves social hierarchies: Rituals specify different treatment for different kinds of people, depending on rank (as opposed to practices that are meant to treat everyone equally). As Xunzi puts it, "The exemplary person has been civilized by these things, and he will also be fond of ritual distinctions. What is mean by 'distinctions'? I say that these refer to gradations of rank according to nobility or baseness, differences between the treatment of old and young, and modes of identification to match these with poverty and wealth and relative [social] importance" (19.3). Rituals involve people with different power in common social practices that treat people differently. But why does Xunzi affirm that rituals must be hierarchical? At one level, he recognizes the social fact of hierarchy and that hierarchical rituals can help to secure social peace: By allotting different responsibilities, privileges, and goods to different individuals, rituals help to prevent conflict over these things among people with different social status.[25] But it's not just a matter of pacifying the potential malcontents and justifying a system that gives more goods to those with more power. Quite the opposite: Hierarchical rituals are essential for generating a sense of community and the emotional disposition for the powerful to care for the interests of those at the bottom of hierarchies.

Like other Confucians, Xunzi intended to persuade political rulers to adopt his ideas because such rulers had the most power to transform society in the desired way. In an ideal society, the wise and humane ruler would implement such rituals, and the whole society would be harmonious and prosperous. But what about nonideal society? Xunzi is famously sensitive to context, and he advocated different prescriptions for different contexts. So the question is how to persuade the rulers who have yet to be morally transformed? For such purposes, Xunzi had to appeal to their self-interest. The problem, however, is that the powerful have the most to benefit from "uncivilized" society, where the strong can rely on brute force to exploit the weak. Those with power need to be persuaded that they benefit from a social system that seems to place constraints on their desires. Hence, much of Xunzi's discussion of ritual is designed to persuade political rulers that it is in their interest to promote rituals in society. Ritual, he says, is the root of the strength of the state (15.8), and the right sort of music can strengthen its military forces (20.5). One would expect rulers to be receptive to this sort of advice.

But rituals do not only benefit rulers. Both Marxists and liberal democrats have denounced hierarchical rituals because they seem designed to benefit the ruling classes of feudal societies and thus are inappropriate for modern times. But this is a misreading of Xunzi's intentions. For Xunzi, hierarchical rituals also have the effect of benefiting the weak and the poor, those who would fare worse in a "state of nature": "Without rituals, desires are unlimited, leading to contention, leading to disorder, and leading to poverty" (19.1). Of course, the tyrant himself won't be the worst hit by a system where he can exercise power without constraints. It is the weak and vulnerable who are worst hit by disorder and poverty: In a situation without ritual civility, Xunzi says, "the strong would harm the weak as well as rob them" (23.9). Putting ritual in practice means "being kind to the humble" (27.17).

But why does Xunzi emphasize rituals involving people with different power? Hierarchical rituals seem most attractive if they are contrasted with practices that exclude people of different status: The rich and powerful do their own thing, as do the poor and the weak (consider the stereotypical account of the Indian caste system, or the different rituals of the rich and the poor in highly stratified societies such as the United States). The choice, typically, is not between hierarchical and egalitarian rituals, but between rituals that involve the powerful and the vulnerable and two different sets of rituals for those with power and those without. Xunzi argues for the former. The village wine ceremony, for example, is praised because the (less powerful) young and (more powerful) old take a drink from the same wine cup, and "in this way we know it is possible for junior and senior to drink together without anyone being left out" (20.12). Rituals such as common birth, marriage, and burial practices also have the effect of including the poor and marginalized as part of the society's culture and common understandings. As Patricia Buckley Ebrey puts it, "Confucian texts and the rituals based on them did not simply convey social distinctions. At another level they overcome them by fostering commonalities in the ways people performed rituals. . . . [In early modern Europe, by contrast], over time class differences in the performance of family rituals seem to have narrowed rather than widened."[26] In hierarchical rituals, the powerful are made to think of the powerless as part of the group, and they are more likely to do things for them (or at least, to refrain from the worst parts of rapacious behavior).

It is no coincidence that Xunzi devotes a great deal of attention to the proper treatment of the dead, notwithstanding his aversion to religious thinking and supernatural explanations for changes in the world of the living. The dead, for obvious reasons, are the least capable of protecting their interests. They are the worst off of the worst off. Hence, those with power—the living— need to be trained by means of certain rituals to treat them with respect. Xunzi carefully specifies the need to adorn the corpse because "if the corpse is not adorned, it becomes hideous, and if it is hideous, no grief will be felt" (19.12). He also specifies that the corpse must be gradually moved farther away each time it is adorned because "if it is kept close at hand, one begins to scorn it; when having it close at hand makes it the object of scorn, one begins to weary of it; when one wearies of it, one forgets one's duty to it; and if one forgets one's duties, then one no longer shows proper respect" (19.12). The ritual should be gradually phased out so that it allows for a smooth transition to everyday life as well as an extension of the cultivated emotions of proper respect and mindfulness of duty to the needy in the world of the living: "With each move he takes it further away, whereby he ensures continued respect. With the passage of time he resumes the ordinary course of life, whereby he cares for the needs of the living" (19.12).

The real moral value of hierarchical rituals, for Xunzi, is that they generate a sense of community among people with different power and status, and benefit both the powerful and the weak. Put differently, they can help to generate a sense of strong reciprocity among members of a hierarchical relationship, with both the powerful and the weak coming to think of their fate as a common one.[27] The bonds that hold them together are stronger than the fluctuating interests that underpin "weak reciprocity."

Xunzi did not only have "domestic policy" in mind. Hierarchical rituals can work their magic not just between people in one country, but also between people in different countries.[28]

Xunzi is particularly critical of economic diplomacy between states on the grounds that it can, at most, generate a weak sense of reciprocity that breaks down once the states' interests are no longer aligned:

> If you serve them with wealth and treasure, then wealth and treasure will run out and your relations with them will still not be normalized. If agreements are sealed and alliances confirmed by oath, then though the agreements be fixed yet they will not last a day. If you cut off borderland to bribe them, then after it is cut off they will be avaricious for yet more. The more you pander to them, the more they will advance on you until you have used up your resources and the state has given over and then there is nothing left.[29]

If a rich country aims to gain friends just by throwing money at them, those friends will be fickle indeed.

That said, Xunzi does not deny that "weak reciprocity" grounded in mutually beneficial self-interest between hierarchical powers can be relatively stable and long lasting. In an anarchic world of self-interested states, what Xunzi calls the "hegemonic state" (霸) can attain interstate leadership by being strategically reliable:

> Although virtue may not be up to the mark, nor were norms fully realized, yet when the principle of all under heaven is somewhat gathered together, punishments and rewards are already trusted by all under heaven, all below the ministers know what they can expect. Once administrative commands are made plain, even if one sees one's chances for gain defeated, yet there is no cheating the people; contracts are already sealed, even if one sees one's chance for gain defeated, yet there is no cheating one's partners. If it is so, then the troops will be strong and the town will be firm and enemy

states will tremble in fear. Once it is clear the state stands united, your allies will trust you. . . . This is to attain hegemony by establishing strategic reliability.[30]

But strategic reliability must also have a basis in hard power for the hegemon to gain the trust of its allies. A very poor or weak country cannot be trusted to keep its promises. So with a combination of wealth, military might, and strategic reliability, a self-interested but honest hegemon can establish mutually beneficial interest-based relations with weaker states. If China's "belt and road initiative" provides material benefits both to China and to weaker countries in Central Asia, and China sticks to its contracts even in economically difficult times and shows that it's a trustworthy partner, the initiative can be successful in the short to medium term. Let's call this relation "weak reciprocity plus"—grounded in nothing more than the self-interest of states, but more stable than Kautilyan-style peace pacts or naked economic diplomacy.

The most stable (and desirable) kind of international leadership, however, is what Xunzi calls "humane authority" (王), meaning a ruler who wins the hearts of the people at home and abroad. At home, the proper use of rituals, combined with effective policies that secure peace and prosperity, is key to leadership success: "one who cultivates ritual becomes a humane authority; one who effectively exercises government becomes strong."[31] Setting a good model at home is necessary but not sufficient. The humane authority can gain the hearts of those abroad by institutionalizing interstate rituals:

If you want to deal with the norms between small and large, strong and weak states to uphold them prudently, then rituals and customs must be especially diplomatic, the jade disks

should be especially bright, and the diplomatic gifts particularly rich, the spokespersons should be gentlemen who write
elegantly and speak wisely. If they keep the people's interests
at heart, who will be angry with them? If they are so, then the
furious will not attack. One who seeks his reputation is not
so. One who seeks profit is not so. One who acts out of anger
is not so. The state will be at peace, as if built on a rock and it
will last long like the stars.[32]

Moreover, the content of the rituals depends on the hierarchy
of states: "The norms of humane authority are to observe the
circumstances so as to produce the tools to work thereon, to
weigh the distance and determine the tribute due. How could
it then be equal!"[33] The Western Zhou dynasty—regarded by
Confucian thinkers as the ideal humane authority—set the
model for hierarchical rituals with surrounding states with its
system of Five Services:

> Therefore, the various Chinese states had the same service and
> the same customs, whereas the states of the Man, Yi, Di, and
> Rong had the same service but different regulations. Within
> the pale was the domain service and outside the pale the feu-
> dal service. The feudal areas up to the border area were the
> tributary service; the Man and the Yi were in the formal ser-
> vice; the Rong and the Di were in the wasteland service. The
> domain service sacrificed to the king's father, the feudal ser-
> vice sacrificed to the king's grandparents, the tributary service
> sacrificed to the king's ancestors, the formal service presented
> tribute, and the wasteland service honored the king's acces-
> sion. The sacrifices to the father were carried out daily, to the
> grandfather monthly, to the ancestors by season. The tribute
> was offered once a year. This is what is called observing the

circumstances so as to produce the tools to work thereon, weighing the distance, and determining the tribute due. This is the system of humane authority.[34]

The general principle, as Yan Xuetong explains, is that "the norm [ritual] of providing offerings at different frequencies was made according to geographic distance from the throne."[35] At one level, the principle of greater reciprocity among closer political communities was an accommodation to the practical reality of the difficulties of traveling long distances at the time. But geography also matters because territorial proximity generates more security threats. A large powerful country can afford to be "neutral" (to borrow in Kautilya's terminology): It can provide security guarantees to surrounding states and peaceful conditions beneficial to all sides in the hierarchical relationship, hence meeting the requirements of weak reciprocity grounded in mutual self-interest. But territorial proximity between a strong state and its weaker neighbors also allows for more frequent rituals and interactions between people, hence providing the basis for long-lasting harmonious relations that help neighboring states weather the changing conceptions of self-interest. We are closer to strong reciprocity grounded in common values and mutual learning.

Such speculation is not mere theory: The ideal of reciprocity between hierarchical political communities informed the tributary system in imperial China, with the Middle Kingdom at the center and "peripheral" states on the outside. In this system, the tributary ruler or his representative had to go to China to pay homage in ritual acknowledgment of his vassal status. In return, China guaranteed security and provided economic benefits.[36] In Ming China, the surrounding political communities were divided into five zones corresponding to the Five Services system of Western Zhou, and the frequency of ritual interaction (roughly) correlated with the degree of closeness to the center (capital) of China, which was also meant to map the cultural achievement. What's interesting for our purposes is that the system allowed for both weak and strong reciprocity. The security guarantees to the surrounding states allowed for peaceful relations that benefited both China and the vassal states. Students of Korean and Vietnamese history will know that there were repeated incursions/invasions from China, but the big picture was relatively peaceful (again, in comparison to similar periods in European history): According to David Kang, there was only one war between Korea, Japan, and China in five centuries of the tributary system in the Ming and Qing dynasties.[37] And what's even more interesting is that borders were respected even without the notion of respect for the sovereignty of equal states: The borders between Korea, Japan, Vietnam, and China were relatively fixed and did not significantly change during those five centuries. The comparison with European imperialism is even more striking in terms of the dynamic of economic relations. Whereas European imperialism was motivated partly, if not mainly, by the quest for profit, the tribute-trade system was a net loss for China and generally benefited the tributary.[38] The imbalance between tribute received and gifts bestowed helped maintain the hierarchical East Asian political order centered on China because it made Chinese vassals understandably eager to have their inferior status recognized, thus entitling them to receive tribute.[39] Salvatore Babones comments that "the emperor could even punish vassals by refusing to receive tribute from them—a 'punishment' that makes sense only in terms of the disproportionate benefits accruing to the tribute-giver."[40] Clearly these hierarchical relations satisfy the conditions for weak reciprocity, since they were mutually beneficial, and in some ways even more beneficial to the weaker surrounding states.

More controversially, the tributary system also allowed for a certain degree of strong reciprocity between hierarchically ordered states. China used moral power to spread Confucian norms, while allowing traditional ways of life and practices to flourish.[41] Korea, Vietnam, and (to a lesser extent) Japan willingly accepted Chinese ideas and institutions (such as the examination system) and sought to model themselves on China.[42] This is not to deny that instrumental considerations motivated most of the interaction between states in the tributary system, but Zhang Feng's empirical analysis found that the early Ming's foreign relations with Korea, Japan, and Mongolia were motivated by expressive considerations in accordance with Confucian propriety—a form of what we term "strong reciprocity"— about one-fifth of the time.[43]

Of course, even weak reciprocity was frequently violated in practice. In a study on the Ming dynasty's grand strategy against the Mongols, Alasdair Ian Johnston is struck by "the prevalence of assumptions and decision axioms that in fact placed a high degree of value on the use of pure violence to resolve security conflicts."[44] Others argue that the tributary system itself is largely an invention of Western sinologists and cannot usefully explain China's interaction with its neighbors over long periods of time.[45] In historical practice, Chinese imperial courts did not usually use the idea of tributary relations to interfere in the internal affairs of neighboring states, and the states on China's periphery often had complete independence to do as they wished: The tributary system, according to Zhuang Guotu, was an "unreality."[46]

Even assuming a large gap between the ideal and the reality of the tributary system in imperial China, however, it doesn't follow that the ideal is not worth defending today. On the face of it, the tributary system seems like a good recipe for hierarchical relations between a strong power and weaker surrounding states.

The central power offers material benefits and security guarantees to weaker surrounding states, and the weaker states pay sym-
bolic tribute to the leadership of the central power, with frequency of ritualistic interaction depending on geographical
distance from the central power. Such an arrangement can be
mutually beneficial, and rituals can help generate a sense of community between the strong and the weak states: what we have
termed "strong reciprocity." So should China try to re-establish
the tributary system with surrounding countries today? Yan Xuetong answers firmly in the negative: "any effort to restore the
tribute system will weaken China's capability for international
political mobilization."[47] But why not try?

3. One World, Two Hierarchical Systems?

Whatever its advantages in the past, the tributary system is
problematic for the modern world, even as an ideal. The most
obvious reason is that the tributary system, which symboli-
cally enshrines the secondary status and moral inferiority of the
vassal states, is incompatible with the idea of the equality of
sovereign states. In reality, as mentioned, states are neither sovereign nor equal, but there may be a case for paying lip service
to the ideal of equal sovereignty even knowing it's far removed
from the reality (and knowing it cannot become anywhere close
to the reality in the foreseeable future). The argument for hypocrisy has a long history in political theory.[48] For example,
Plato (in *The Republic*) famously defended the idea of a "noble
lie" to persuade those at the bottom of the political hierarchy to
endorse an ideal republic run by philosopher kings and queens.
The religious skeptic David Hume mounted a vigorous case in
defense of an established church on the grounds that it is essential for social order.[49] Xunzi most likely did not believe that

the human performance of rituals could have the power to affect supernatural beings such as ghosts or spirits, but he still defends religious rituals because of their positive psychological
and social effects.[50] Today, Straussian political theorists know-
ingly propagate what they consider to be falsehoods such as the
idea of natural rights on the grounds that they are necessary to
pacify the poorly educated masses who can't deal with disturbing philosophical truths that cast doubt on the ultimate value of
their ordinary way of life. Arguably, a similar case can be made for
paying lip service to the ideal of the equality of sovereign states.
Notwithstanding a history of informal bullying by powerful
countries, it has served to constrain legal takeover of territory in
the post–World War II era. Over the past few decades, China
has become distinctly obsessed with sovereignty in the form of
noninterference in the internal affairs of countries precisely
because it seeks to avoid a repeat of seeing its territory carved
up by foreign powers.

That said, there are limits to the idea of paying lip service to
sovereignty. Most obviously, rulers lose the moral right to govern if they engage in massive abuses of basic human rights of
their own people. Earlier Confucian thinkers such as Mencius
defended the view that what we'd call today "humanitarian intervention" can be justified if the aim is to liberate people who
are being oppressed by tyrants,[51] and the Chinese government
has recently signed up to the international accord that enshrines
the "responsibility to protect" people from genocide and systematic violations of basic human rights.[52] Secondly, the ideal
of equality of sovereign states should not be used by powerful
countries as an excuse to shirk their extra share of responsibility
for dealing with global challenges. If we agree that justice requires political leaders to take into account the interests of all
those affected by their policies, then political leaders in large

powerful countries have a responsibility to consider how their policies affect not just the current generation of people in the home country, but also future generations, people in other countries, and the natural world. If large countries launch major wars or make "mistakes" on such issues as climate change and artificial intelligence, it can literally be the end of the world. As one author recently put it, China "shakes the world;"[53] in contrast, nobody would write a book titled *Canada Shakes the World*. So it would be frankly immoral if leaders of large countries proclaim that they look out only for the interests of their own people; even President Trump claims that he defends the principle of "American first" rather than "America alone."[54] In short, it's fine to pay (hypocritical) lip service to the ideal of sovereign equal states, but large states should not use that as an excuse to shirk what ought to be an extra share of global responsibilities.

There's another fatal flaw with the proposal to re-establish the tributary system in the modern world: Today, powerful countries are not necessarily the most civilized (or advanced), from a moral point of view. The tributary system was founded on the assumption that China is the center of culture and morality, and that China can and should spread its superior civilization to the rest of the world. The closer the country (or "zone") to Beijing (the capital in the Ming and Qing dynasties), the more civilized the territory, and conversely, the farther away from Beijing, the more wild the barbarians. Nobody seriously holds this view today. That's not to deny the value of proximity to powerful countries. Kautilya's worry that territorial contiguity can generate conflicts still holds true today, so major powers need to establish mutually beneficial peace pacts with neighboring countries: For example, strong countries can provide nuclear guarantees to neighboring states on the condition that those states do not manufacture their own nuclear weapons. Proximity also allows for more frequent interaction—ritual and otherwise—hence providing the conditions for a stronger form of reciprocity grounded in common values, similar to Ashoka's effort to promote Buddhist-inspired values to neighboring states and the spread of Confucianism from China to Korea and Vietnam. In short, the challenge is to reconstitute a *de facto* form of hierarchy between strong states and neighboring (weaker) states that provides the conditions for weak and (ideally) strong reciprocity while still paying lip service to the ideal of equal sovereignty of states.

A modernized version of the traditional Chinese ideal of *tianxia*, conventionally translated as "all-under-heaven,"[55] can inspire thinking about a hierarchical system of states that is both realistic and desirable. The term *tianxia* is a vague concept that has been used differently in different times (and differently in the same times).[56] In the Tang dynasty, for example, *tianxia* referred either to the area actually governed by Tang dynasty rulers or the whole world with *Zhongguo* (China) at its core surrounded by other countries.[57] To further complicate matters, the term has sometimes been used in a descriptive sense meaning territory and other times in a normative sense of an ideal that contrasts with the reality. In the Mencius, for example, the term is used eighty-six times[58] and often refers to an ideal of a unified world without any territorial boundaries governed by one benevolent ruler, an ideal that is meant to contrast with the ugly reality of small states competing ruthlessly for territorial advantage in the Warring States period.

In contemporary times, *tianxia* was famously revived by the philosopher Zhao Tingyang who gave it a normative definition. According to Zhao's formulation, *tianxia* has three meanings: (1) a geographical meaning referring to the whole world; (2) a psychological meaning in the sense that the hearts of all the world's peoples are unified, like a big family; and (3) an institutional meaning in the sense of a world government with the power to ensure universal order.[59] Critics in the West have raised doubts about this project. William Callahan, for example, has charged that Zhao's ideal of *tianxia* masks an effort to replace Western hegemony with Chinese hegemony.[60] But Zhao is explicitly committed to a hierarchically organized cosmopolitan ideal. Institutionally, he argues for a world organization that would have more territory and resources than any one state (including the Chinese state): "The world government directly rules a land called King-land, about twice the size of a large sub-state, and four times that of a medium sized sub-state and so on. The military force controlled by the world government is greater than that of large, medium and small sub-states with a ration of 6 to 3, 6 to 2, and 6 to 1 divisions. This proportional design limits the King-land of the world government in its advantages over the sub-states either in resources or military power."[61] The problem, however, is that Zhao's interpretation of *tianxia* is neither desirable nor realistic.

Zhao claims that his ideal derives inspiration from the values and practices put forward by the founding fathers of the Zhou dynasty approximately three thousand years ago—the same sage kings who inspired Confucius—but his ideal is radically inconsistent with the key Confucian value of graded love. Zhao's global government is supposed to be supported by the world's people psychologically bound like an intimate family,[62] but this ideal owes more to Mohism and imported traditions like Buddhism, Christianity, Marxism, and liberal cosmopolitanism that aim to break down particularistic attachments. Every Chinese intellectual knows the famous passage from the *Great Learning*—a Han dynasty work subsequently canonized by the

Song dynasty scholar Zhu Xi (1130–1200) as one of the four Confucian classics—that lays out the road to *tianxia*: "when the personal life is cultivated, the family will be regulated; when the family is regulated, the state will be in order; and when the state is in order, there is peace throughout the world (*tianxia*)." Starting from the moral ordering of the individual person and the family, an important goal of Confucianism is to bring order to the state and thereby spread peace throughout the world. The ideal is a harmonious political order of global peace. But nowhere does the *Great Learning* state that ties to the people outside the state should be as strong as, or stronger than, ties to people within the state. The reason is simple: Ties should be extended from intimates to others, but with diminishing intensity as we move beyond the circle of intimates. We owe more to intimates (starting with the family) than to strangers, both because they are the main sources of happiness and because we need to reciprocate for what they have done to us. In other words, the key social relations do not matter equally: Our ethical obligations are strongest to those with whom we have personal relationships, and they diminish in intensity the farther we go from those relationships. We do have an obligation to extend love beyond intimates, but it is not expected that the same degree of emotions and responsibilities will extend to strangers. The web of caring obligations that binds family members is more demanding than that binding citizens, the web of obligations that bind citizens is more demanding than that binding foreigners, and the web binding humans is more demanding than that binding us to nonhuman forms of life. The ideal of graded love is not meant to deny that we have obligations to the wider world. Just as we should extend ties beyond the family, so too should we extend ties beyond the nation. Extending this concern to outsiders, although with less concern as they extend further and further from the political community, is also natural and right. Hence, Confucians should not just view special concern for fellow citizens as a politically necessary compromise or a second-best deviation from an ideal world. Nor is it just a necessary step on the way to the politics of global love and government. At least some sort of special commitment to the political community is required by the logic of graded love, a commitment that should be extended (in diminishing degrees) to outsiders. Zhao's interpretation of *tianxia*, in short, has it backward: Attachments to particular political communities should have ethical and political priority over attachments to the world. We do need to think about obligations to the world, but not if it entails systematically overriding obligations to particularistic attachments.

The second problem with Zhao's interpretation of *tianxia* is that he doesn't provide any plausible mechanism for realizing his ideal. As Zhang Feng puts it, "the critical flaw of Zhao's thesis is his failure to outline any clear pathway that might lead to the creation of the world institutions of the *tianxia* system. . . . He insists on the priority of the world institution, yet surprisingly fails to provide any description of how it might come about . . . and [be] maintained."[63] Zhang wrote these words in 2010, and with the rise of nationalist populism the gap between Zhao's ideal and the reality has further widened, almost to the point of no return.

But we can reformulate Zhao's ideal so that it is both realistic and desirable: All we have to do is change "the world" to "East Asia" and defend the ideal of attachment to the East Asian region without the implication that this attachment needs to override ethical and political attachments to the state (or other "lower" forms of communal attachments, such as attachment to the family). So here's the reformulation of the *tianxia* ideal: (1) a geographical meaning referring to East Asia; (2) a psychological meaning in the sense that the hearts of the East Asian peoples are unified, minimally in the sense of weak reciprocity, with an aspiration for strong reciprocity; and (3) an institutional meaning in the sense of a hierarchical East Asian political order led by China that pays lip service to the ideal of the equal sovereignty of states. On this modernized account of *tianxia*, China is the center of East Asia by virtue of its dominant economic status and increasing ability to project military power, and it has both extra powers and extra responsibilities in the East Asian region. In practice, it might mean setting up East Asian regional institutions with China as the major power, similar, perhaps, to Germany's role in the European Union. As a nuclear state, China can give security guarantees and economic benefits to weaker states such as North Korea in exchange for nuclear disarmament. It might mean common East Asian financial institutions (or even a common currency), with China as the major player accompanied by the responsibility to bail out weaker states in times of economic crisis. And the more flexible (or hypocritical) approach to sovereignty might actually contribute to solving territorial disputes with China's neighbors because China's leaders might place less emphasis on the sanctity of territorial boundaries: As Allen Carlson puts it, "In a reconstituted *tianxia* system, the territorial and jurisdictional concerns which have so preoccupied China's leaders over the course of the last century could be re-imagined as issues involving peripheral regions, not zero-sum disputes over sovereign recognition. In this sense, a *tianxia* order might pave the way for novel solution of such controversies, and as such lead to greater stability in the region." The problem, as Carlson recognizes, is that states along China's periphery are likely to construe an attempt to impose (or even articulate) a new normative hierarchical order in the East Asian region as a threat: "Within such a system it is clear that China is to occupy the paramount position, while those along its margins are expected to accept such dominance and show fealty to the center."[64] But China's "peripheral" states need not show fealty in any official sense (hence the key difference with the tributary system), as long as they usually defer to the major power (China) on issues of global significance.

Such arrangements seem unlikely now, but stranger things have happened: Who could have imagined the EU in the midst of World War II? And, unlike Europe, the long history of an East Asian region with China as the center could provide a psychological basis for reestablishment and maintenance of attachment to an East Asian region led by China. Still, it must be recognized that China's neighbors such as South Korea, Japan, and Vietnam—the same countries that were tightly integrated in the China-led tributary system—seem distinctly worried by China's growing economic and military might.

So how could China regain the trust of its neighbors? Obviously a bellicose approach to solving regional disputes cannot be effective in the long term. At the end of the day, China must set a good model at home. As Yan Xuetong puts it, "For China to become a superpower modeled on humane authority, it must first become a model from which other states are willing to learn."[65] As regional leader, China would also try to provide neighboring states with mutual benefits that underpin weak reciprocity. At minimum, it means securing the peace. Whatever we think of China's foreign policy, the fact that it has not launched any wars since 1979 should be a source of comfort. But China should aim for more. Ideally, it would provide the conditions for strong reciprocity by relying on such means as Ashoka-style respectful and restrained speech and Xunzi-style common rituals that generate a sense of community. Unlike the tributary system, which involved China teaching its supposed cultural and moral inferiors, the learning curve would work both ways, with "periph-eral" states learning from Chinese culture and China learning from neighboring states. The deepest ties between states in a hi-erarchical system are underpinned by the strongest possible form of reciprocity.

From a *realpolitik* point of view, the United States' military hegemony in the East Asian region is perhaps the main ob-stacle to the development of an East Asian *tianxia* hierarchy led by China.[66] But things could change. North Korea is cur-rently the major military threat in the East Asian region, but it is possible that the divided Korean peninsula will unify over the next few decades in some form or another. At that point, there would be a weaker case for United States' troops in the East Asian region, and a unified Korea would fall under the "natural" influence of China due to its proximity and superior power in East Asia.[67] China need not (and should not) send troops to Korea to replace the Americans, but it could provide security guarantees to Korea, such as protection against inva-sion by neighboring countries. This kind of scenario may not appeal to Koreans in favor of full sovereignty, but sometimes less powerful countries need to make the best of less-than-ideal solutions. Canada, for example, was invaded twice by its more powerful southern neighbor (in 1775 and 1812, before Canada became an independent country), and still today many Canadians take pride in being different from Ameri-cans. But Canadians know they are a small country (in terms of population and global influence), and the government usually refrains from doing things that antagonize the bigger and more powerful southern neighbor. Canada can occasionally object to U.S. foreign policy (for example, the Canadian parliament objected to the 2003 invasion of Iraq), but Canadians would never dream today of, say, inviting the British (or the Chinese) to build military bases in Canada as a buffer against the United States. Such arrangements also benefit the weaker party: Good ties with the Americans are valuable for Canadians because Canada does not have to spend much on the military, with the consequence that the Canadian government can devote more resources to improving the welfare of the Canadian people. So, yes, Canadians are not the equals of Americans on the international stage, but what's the problem if a bit of inequality under the umbrella of an American-led regional *tianxia* arrangement benefits the Canadian people?[68]

Still, it could be argued that American military bases in the East Asian region are really meant to check China's rise. China may well become the biggest economic power in the world over the next few decades, with more demands for status and global influence, and perhaps the United States has no intention of reducing its military influence in the East Asian region. This kind of attitude can lead to a disastrous war between two major powers. Jonathan Renshon demonstrates empirically that states attributed less status than they are due based on material capabilities are overwhelmingly more likely (than "satisfied" states) to initiate militarized disputes.[69] The policy implication should be obvious: "conflict may be avoided through status concessions before the escalation to violent conflict occurs."[70] Renshon has Russia in mind, but exactly the same point applies in the case of China: If the United States genuinely wants to avoid war in the East Asian region, it should try to accommodate and make concessions to China's desire to establish a regional hierarchy with itself at the head of the table. In the 1970s, the United States did courageously cut its official diplomatic ties to Taiwan in order to recognize the preeminent role of China in the East Asian region, and it should make more such concessions in the future.

In short, the most viable path toward global peace in the region involves a bipolar world with the United States and China as heads of two regional hierarchies of states that also benefit the weaker states in the hierarchical relationships. Both China and the United States recognize each other's leadership in their respective regions, and they work together to solve common global problems such as climate change. But why should other major regional powers such as the EU and Russia accept such an arrangement? The most important reason is that too many global leaders would make it more difficult to coordinate peaceful relations and work on joint global projects. It's fine if Russia and the EU are recognized as less-than-major powers with more say in their own neighborhoods, but they can't be equals with China and the United States on the world stage. There must be a hierarchy of regional hierarchical systems.

Perhaps the biggest challenge will be to accommodate India. The country's rate of economic growth has recently overtaken China's, and India may well achieve rough parity with China in terms of population and global clout over the next few decades.[71] So how can the two countries work together? The situation may not look promising now (the two countries were on the brink of another border war in 2017 and China's closest partner in South Asia is Pakistan, India's less-than-friendly neighbor). Again, we need to invoke Kautilya's insight that two countries with contiguous borders often regard each other as natural enemies. China and India went to war in 1962, and they have yet to resolve their territorial conflicts (in contrast, China has peacefully resolved territorial conflicts with eleven of its other neighboring countries). But the two countries were both members of the nonaligned movement during the Cold War, and today China is India's biggest trading partner, thus underpinning mutually beneficial relations of weak reciprocity. Ties between India and

China have been improving since early 2018—China's President Xi Jinping suggested that "shared Asian values" should trump the geopolitical differences between the two countries—and India has emerged as the biggest beneficiary of the Chinese-led Asian Infrastructure Investment Bank.[72] Past history also points the way to a stronger form of reciprocity that underpins lasting peace.[73] Buddhism spread peacefully from India to China, to the point that it has become far more influential in China. In the 1920s, the poet Tagore deeply marked Chinese intellectual culture when he visited China.[74] The great Chinese intellectual Liang Shuming regarded Indian spiritual culture as the apex of human moral growth.[75] And the learning was mutual: India benefited from China's paper, gunpowder, and silk. Perhaps China's greatest gift to India, according to Amitav Acharya, was the preservation of Buddhist texts. Chinese and Indian translators lived and worked in China and translated and preserved Buddhist texts. After Buddhism disappeared in India and original Indian texts were lost or destroyed by invaders, these Chinese translations preserved Buddhist *sutras*, which could then be retranslated for Indians.[76] Buddhism would have been lost to Indians without Chinese help, just as Arabs preserved Greek texts in science and philosophy that would otherwise have been lost.

Of course, some differences between China and India, such as different ways of selecting political leaders, need to be respected. But such differences pale compared to what ought to be deep mutual respect between two countries with thousands of years of history and such glorious and diverse civilizations. Given that India and China had ties of strong reciprocity in the past, how might it be possible to reestablish such ties in the future? Once again, we need to turn to the insights of ancient thinkers. If the leaders of the two great Asian powers follow Ashoka's guidelines for respectful and restrained speech and implement Xunzi's ideas for rituals that generate a sense of community, their diplomatic, cultural, and people-to-people interactions might well (re)generate a strong sense of reciprocity. It is not impossible to image a future world with an Asian hierarchical system jointly led and managed by India and China, to the benefit of both countries, surrounding smaller states, and perhaps even the whole world.[77]

But the whole world includes not just humans: We also need to consider our relations with the animal kingdom. In the following chapter, we argue that hierarchical relations with animals can be morally justified if they are characterized by the principle of subordination without cruelty, though this principle can and should be interpreted differently based on different kinds of animals and the relation we (humans) have with them.

4

Just Hierarchy between Humans and Animals

SUBORDINATION WITHOUT CRUELTY

When the stables burned down, Confucius was at court. On his return, he asked "Was anyone hurt?" He did not ask about the horses.

—*THE ANALECTS OF CONFUCIUS*, 10.14

WE SPEND MOST of our time thinking about the obligations we owe to other human beings. Our news outlets report mainly on the horrors committed by some human beings against other human beings and few shed tears over, say, the number of innocent animals killed in devastating earthquakes. But we live in a natural world that sustains our way of life, and we interact with animals that enrich our lives and make them meaningful. Try to imagine a world without animals: no pets, no birds in the sky, fish in the sea, or safaris in Zambia. Even if it were feasible to sustain human life without animals, it would be an infinitely depressing place! So we need to ask about our proper relation with animals. The traditional view—in Western societies—is that humans are on top of a moral hierarchy, with the power to dominate animals. But this view has been increasingly rejected of late. Many contemporary thinkers defend the principle that animals are our equals and should be treated as such. We defend the traditional view. But affirming a hierarchy between animals and humans doesn't justify cruelty against animals. When it comes to the treatment of animals, we defend the principle of subordination without cruelty. But that principle is not sufficient to spell out the kinds of obligations we owe to animals. We have different relations with different kinds of animals, and we owe stronger obligations of care to animals that share human-like traits and contribute most to our well-being. At the other end of the spectrum, we owe least to ugly animals that harm humans, but the principle of subordination without cruelty applies even in the case of nasty cockroaches.

1. Are Animals Our Equals?

The modernization and industrialization of Western societies has been largely beneficial for human members of those societies. Karl Marx's contemptuous dismissal of the "rural idiocy" of village life in India, where the natives worshiped cows and monkeys rather than dedicating themselves to self-emancipation,[1] may be an expression of racism and Eurocentrism, but not many of us would want to return to the days of grinding poverty, limited horizons, and outdoor toilets.[2] The flip side of modernization, especially as it has spread to the rest of the world, is the toll it has taken on the animal kingdom. The human population has doubled since the 1960s, while wild animal populations have dropped by nearly a third. Over 56 billion animals are killed per year for food (not including aquatic animals), and meat production is expected to double again by 2050.³ Marx himself would probably blame capitalism—the relentless quest for profit comes at the cost of habitats lost and animals consumed for the sake of satisfying endless human desires. If corporations need to sacrifice cows and monkeys for the sake of selling things to greedy human beings, then that's the price of capitalism.

But cows have been largely spared in India because they are viewed as sacred by the majority of Hindu worshipers, even in modernized parts of the country. So capitalism *per se* is not sufficient to explain the annihilation of animal species in recent times: Lack of concern for animal welfare in the economic realm must be supported and reinforced by cultural and religious ideas that view animals as mere means for human well-being. In Western societies, arguably, the main ideological culprit has been the Christian religion. The dominant official Christian doctrine has excluded animals from consideration as having souls and has stressed the Old Testament pronouncements that gave humans the power to rule over the animal kingdom: "Then God said, "Let us make mankind in his image, in our likeness, so that they may rule over the fish in the sea and the birds in the sky, over the livestock and all the wild animals, and over all the creatures that move along the ground."⁴ The fate of animals took a turn for the worse in the seventeenth century with the theory of "animal-machines" put forward by René Descartes, one of the pioneers of the scientific revolution and the mechanistic vision of the natural world. According to Descartes, not only do animals exist for the benefit of humans, but, in addition, they feel nothing:

> Animals are mere machines, automatons. They feel neither pleasure, nor pain, nor anything else. Although they can emit cries when we cut them with knives, or contort themselves in

their efforts to avoid contact with a hot-iron, it doesn't mean that they feel pain in those situations. They are governed by the same principles as a clock, and if their actions are more complex than those of a clock, it's because these are machines built by humans, while animals are infinitely more complex machines, made by God.[5]

Such wrong-headed views justified acts of unimaginable cruelty carried out in the name of the pursuit of scientific truth. As Gary Francione explains, "Descartes and his followers performed experiments in which they nailed animals by their paws onto boards and cut them open to reveal their beating hearts. They burned, scalded, and mutilated animals in every conceivable manner. When the animals reacted as though they were suffering pain, Descartes dismissed the reaction as no different from the sound of a machine that was functioning improperly. A crying dog, Descartes maintained, is no different from a whining gear that needs oil."[6]

Not surprisingly, there was a counterreaction to these views. A few decades later, Voltaire expressed outrage at such practices: "Barbarians seize the dog, who wins so prodigiously over man in terms of friendship; they nail him on a table, and dissect it alive to show its mezaraic veins. You discover in him *all the same organs of feeling that are in yourself.* Listen to me, mechanist: did nature arrange all the springs of feeling in that animal *so that he doesn't feel anything?* Does he have nerves so he is impassive?"[7] Such disputes came to a head in the nineteenth century. Claude Bernard, the great French physiologist, proclaimed that total disregard of distress and pain in his unanaesthetized animals was the attitude proper for scientists, but his own wife and daughters founded the first antivivisection society in Europe after they came home to find that he had vivisected the domestic dog.[8]

Supporters of animal welfare argued against religious and secular outlooks that seemed to justify cruel treatment of animals. Most famously, the utilitarian thinker Jeremy Bentham argued that we should stop treating the species barrier as crucial, and instead treat all sentient beings as inside the moral community. Just as the French had recently abolished slavery in their colonies:

> The day *may* come when the rest of the animal creation may acquire those rights which never could have been withholden from them but by the hand of tyranny. The French have already discovered that the blackness of the skin is not reason why a human being should be abandoned without redress to the caprice of a tormentor. It may one day come to be recognized that the number of the legs, the villosity of the skin, or the termination of the *os sacrum* are reasons equally insufficient for abandoning a sensitive being to the same fate. What else is it that should trace the insuperable line? Is it the faculty of reason, or perhaps the faculty of discourse? But a full-grown horse or dog is beyond comparison a more rational, as well as more conversable animal, than an infant of a day or a week, or even of a month, old. But suppose they were otherwise, what would it avail? The question is not, Can they *reason*? Nor Can they *talk*? but Can they *suffer*.[9]

The contemporary utilitarian thinker Peter Singer elaborated Bentham's insights into a theory of animal liberation: "All animals are equal [to humans]." Since "the taking into account of the interests of the being, whatever those interests may be— must, according to the principle of equality, be extended to all beings, black or white, masculine or feminine, human or nonhuman" and "the capacity for suffering and enjoyment is a prerequisite for having any interests at all," therefore "if a being suffers

there can be no moral justification for refusing to take that suffering into consideration. No matter what the nature of the being,
the principle of equality requires that its suffering be counted
equally with the like suffering—in so far as rough comparisons
can be made—of any other being."[10]

Singer's theory has been hugely influential—his book *Animal
Liberation* has sold over half a million copies, and it has become
the bible of the animal liberation movement—but it has also
been hugely controversial because he denies the value of sacred
or inviolable human rights. His view that animals are the equals
of humans—combined with the utilitarian maxim that an act or
policy is justified if it can maximize the happiness and reduce the
suffering of the largest number—would seem to justify the killing of babies in a persistent vegetative state or of elderly people
in the advanced stages of a degenerative disease such as Alzheimer's if it promotes happiness and reduces overall suffering
in the human world and the animal kingdom. Singer does accept
that the lives of higher beings—"persons" that have rationality
or self-consciousness—are more important than mere sentient
beings, with the implication that if we came across a child and
a dog drowning and we could only save one, we would be
under a moral obligation to save the child. But for Singer, not all
persons are humans, and some humans are not persons. An
adult chimpanzee can exhibit more self-consciousness, more
personhood, than a newborn human infant. So if we came across
a newborn infant with severe disabilities who had no family and
a mature chimp with complex family and social ties and we could
only save one of them, we might be under an obligation to save
the chimp: "Killing them [infants], therefore, cannot be equated
with killing normal human beings, or any other self-conscious
beings. No infant—disabled or not—has a strong claim to life as
beings capable of seeing themselves as distinct entities existing

over time."[11] Such views radically conflict with the considered intuitions of (most) people in modern societies. Infanticide may have been common in ancient Greece, but it is repulsive today. For one thing, advanced medical care can cure (or improve) some of the disabilities of babies. And we can grow into people with rich social ties: Human beings are not just beings, we are human becomings.[12] Singer is working with a strangely static view of what it means to be a fulfilled and flourishing person. More surprisingly, perhaps, Singer's utilitarian theory may also be inimical to the interests of the billions of animals raised and killed for human consumption in industrial animal farms. Between 1975 and 2000, the number of animals kept in captivity grew from 8 billion to 17 billion. As Torbjorn Tannsjo explains, "the probable explanation of this fact is that there is a causal connection: We hold more animals because we eat them, and because we who eat them become more numerous." If we provide animals in captivity with good living and dying conditions, and they generally live lives worth experiencing, then from the point of view of total hedonistic utilitarianism "they have our interest in raising and eating them to thank for their lives."[13] With utilitarian friends like that, defenders of animal welfare do not need enemies.

To counter views that justify sacrificing the interests of particular animals for some greater good, Sue Donaldson and Will Kymlicka propose a theory of animal rights that is grounded in basic rights. Animals, like humans, should be seen as possessing *inviolable* rights. There are some things that cannot be done to individual animals—like torture, killing, imprisonment, medical experimentation, separation from families—no matter what the benefit to human beings, the majority of animals, or ecosystems. This rights-based approach is a natural extension of the conception of moral equality underpinning the doctrine of human rights, but it is extended to animals as well.[14] It's worth asking, however, if animals really possess human-like inviolable rights? If so, we should feel the same sense of outrage when the basic rights of animals are violated as when the basic rights of humans are violated. It's true that some defenders of human rights write as though they feel the same sense of outrage when the basic rights of animals are violated. For example, Donaldson and Kymlicka compare the initial process of domestication of animals to the "importation of slaves from Africa."[15] Others compare the modern-day attitudes and methods behind society's treatment of animals to the Nazi Holocaust in World War II.[16] Whatever the validity of these comparisons, it would be somewhat odd if they translated into the same sense of outrage when animals and humans are enslaved and massacred. Sometimes we comfort victims of bad luck or evil deeds by the thought that things could have been even worse. But it would be breathtakingly insensitive, if not immoral, to comfort relatives of those murdered during the Holocaust with the thought that millions more chickens are murdered each year for human consumption. But let's concede that defenders of animal rights really do feel the same sense of outrage when the basic rights of animals and humans are violated. If humans and animals possess equal rights, then animal rights advocates should also argue that the same penalties should be meted out to perpetrators of rights violations against humans and animals. Raimond Gaita remarks that he has never met animal rights activists who acted as if they really believed that the slaughter of animals for meat is equivalent to murder.[17] Donaldson and Kymlicka argue for a whole host of radical remedies and policies to protect the rights of animals, but they do not call for life-long imprisonment of animal meat eaters or people who kill insects. They claim that it would be more just and politically effective to connect the treatment of animals more directly to the language of human rights, but it would be neither just nor politically effective if they pushed their argument to its logical conclusion. That's not to say it doesn't make sense to use the language of rights to make the case for animals' welfare, but it definitely doesn't make sense to say that animals and humans have *equal* rights. Put differently, at some basic level even animal rights activists agree that there is a hierarchy of moral concern between humans and animals, with humans at the top of the hierarchy.

These arguments are not merely theoretical. In one recent case, it was deemed necessary to kill a gorilla named Harambe to save a child who had entered its enclosure at the Cincinnati Zoo. Darting Harambe with a tranquilizer gun was judged too risky as the drugs don't take immediate effect, and the act might have enraged the gorilla before sedating him. Peter Singer and Karen Dawn write that "as animal advocates, we don't automatically deem the life of a boy as exponentially more important than that of a fellow primate, and we might have been inclined to risk the tranquilizer in order to save Harambe's life," but even they recognize that "it is easy for us to say, given that it wasn't our child being dragged by a 400-pound gorilla, so we are not eager to blame zoo officials for their choice."[18] It is tempting to argue that such highly unusual cases should not inform everyday ethics about how to treat animals, but policy makers often need to decide whether to value human lives over animal lives. Should electric cars be programmed to swerve away from animals even if it endangers the life of the driver? Should scientists be forced to end all animal experimentation even if, as the Buddhist philosopher and animal advocate Matthieu Ricard recognizes, almost all the medicine we use has been tested on animals?[19] Should governments legislate against massacres of disease-carrying animals? In one recent case, Australian scientists successfully wiped out more than 80 percent of disease-carrying mosquitoes which spread deadly diseases such as dengue fever and Zika.[20] Again, it would seem extremely odd if animal advocates took their rights rhetoric seriously and proposed to charge these scientists with murder.

So we are back to the traditional Christian view that it may be necessary to affirm a moral hierarchy between humans and animals, with humans prioritized in cases of conflict. But this view is not distinctly Christian. *The Analects of Confucius* reports that "when the stables burned down, Confucius was at court. On his return, he asked, 'Was anyone hurt?' He did not ask about the horses" (10.14). Clearly Confucius valued the life of a human being over that of an animal.[21] Such views, in fact, are almost universal. As Mary Midgley puts it, "the natural preference for one's species does exist. It is not, like race-prejudice, a product of culture. It is found in all human cultures, and in cases of real competition it tends to operate very strongly."[22] Still, we can ask if "speciesism" is a good thing. Patriarchy was a near universal social phenomenon in the past, but progressive people in modern societies reject the idea that men can and should dominate over women. In the same vein, domination over animals may be objectionable even if it's widespread. For example, Fred Besthorn objects to a hierarchy of value between "higher" and "lower" life forms because it "establishes justification for the preferential treatment of some species while others may be ignored or, in the case of insects, annihilated."[23] Even insects, he suggests, should be treated as equals. But domination doesn't necessarily justify indifference, much less annihilation. Ethical traditions that prioritize human life over animal life in cases of conflict do not seek to justify cruelty to animals. Quite the opposite. The Christian cosmic vision that grants "high dominion" of human beings created specially in God's image "is a call to bring our highest aspirations for the cosmos in line with God's, a call to exercise the love, power, and creativity of God's image within us toward the end of enabling the total flourishing of God's world. . . . God's call to high dominion is fundamentally incompatible with cruelty to animals, indifference to their suffering, and the conceit that they are here for us to do with as we please."[24] Confucians who justify a hierarchy between humans and animals also object to the suffering of animals: We owe less compassion to animals than to humans in cases of conflict, but we still need to extend compassion to all living creatures (see section 3 of this chapter for more details). It's true that Confucians often compared unrestrained and intemperate "barbarians" to wild animals, but just as "barbarians" can be civilized by moral education, so the Confucian sage can tame wild beasts by music.[25] In principle, wild beasts, like uneducated people, can become less aggressive and more civilized, so we have moral obligations to them as well. Buddhism affirms a cosmological hierarchy between humans and animals—sensible beings are reincarnated according to *karma* accumulated from former lives, and those with less virtue will be reincarnated as animals rather than humans[26]—but all beings ultimately have the same Buddha nature, and Buddhists strongly affirm a commitment to compassion and against cruelty to animals. Stories from the Buddhist tradition suggest that humans with the highest level of compassion might be prepared to sacrifice their own lives to save the lives of animals.[27]

In short, the problem is not that there is a special species bond between human beings. The problem is when that bond translates into cruelty to animals. Humans have a duty to avoid cruelty to animals, both because animals can suffer and because those who are cruel to animals are more likely to be cruel to humans. That said, the need to avoid cruelty is merely the bottom line, and we may also have more positive obligations to some animals. A pet owner should not be indifferent to a pet dog who craves for her attention and affection, even if she does not mean to be cruel. Here we seek inspiration from the Donaldson and Kymlicka theory of animal rights. We reject their idea that humans and animals have equal *negative* rights (not to be killed, tortured, confined, and so on). There is a moral hierarchy between humans and animals, and if it's a question of life and death, humans should have priority. But we accept their idea that we need to specify what *positive* obligations we owe to animals, such as an obligation to respect animal habitats, design our roads and buildings in a way that takes into account of animals' needs, and obligations to care for animals who have become dependent on us. These positive relational duties arise out of our specific relationships with animals, and we owe different kinds of duties to different kinds of animals. Just as we owe different duties to fellow citizens (e.g., free medical care in Canada) as compared to duties to tourists, so we owe different duties to our pets than to visiting rats in our basement. There is, so to speak, a hierarchy of positive duties, with more duties to animals dependent on our care. Let's say a bit more about why exactly we should value our pets, and what special duties may arise from that care.

2. Domesticated Animals: Subordination with Care

It seems intuitively obvious that we owe different duties to different kinds of animals. We owe more to animals with human-like traits such as intelligence, empathy, self-consciousness, and the ability to be aware of themselves as distinct entities with a past and a future, such as chimpanzees and gorillas.[28] If we have to test the efficacy of a new medicine that promises to cure a human illness on an animal, obviously we should choose a rat over an ape. We also owe more to pets that share our lives, even if they are less intelligent and human-like than great apes. But why do we owe more to pets compared to, say, wolves? Wolves are just as intelligent as dogs and suffer just as much from pain.

Donaldson and Kymlicka use the language of citizenship to justify the extra positive duties we owe to animals that partake of our social lives. We owe special obligations to fellow citizens because we should respect people's capacity to form morally significant attachments and relationships, including attachments to particular communities. So relations between citizens are stronger than between citizens and noncitizens: For example, the interests of citizens (but not tourists) should decide whether to build more subways or homes. Donaldson and Kymlicka argue that the citizenship logic is equally compelling and applicable in the case of both humans and animals. Animals, like people, have a degree of "agency"; they have preferences and can "vote with their feet" if they are unhappy.[29] Similar to humans, domesticated animals that live with us and share our lives are best viewed as equal co-citizens in our political community whose interests count in determining our collective good. Some animals should be viewed as temporary visitors or noncitizen denizens (e.g., squirrels in our gardens) equivalent to visiting tourists, others should be viewed as residents of their own political communities whose sovereignty and territory we should respect (e.g., wolves) similar to the way we respect citizens of other countries, and domesticated animals should be viewed as the equivalent of full and equal co-citizens because of the way they have been bred over generations for interdependence with humans. While domesticated animals cannot actively exercise their democratic self-agency because they lack the capacity of speech and for rational reflection, they can be compared to children and mentally disabled persons who have a right to have their

interests included in determining the public good of the community. Concretely, according to Donaldson and Kymlicka, it
means that representatives can and should be appointed to represent the interests of domesticated animals in the political process. Their representatives need to ensure that we respect the
basic citizenship rights of animal co-citizens: They should have
freedom of movement (e.g., dogs should have the right to go to
restaurants, as in France); there should be less use of animal labor
(e.g., dogs should have more free time to play); domesticated
animals should have the equal right to medical care (there should
be some form of animal insurance); they should have the right
to a family (we should not take newborns away from their parents); they should have the right to reside in their own territory
and should not be moved away without their consent (i.e., it's
okay if they leave on their own but they can't be forced to do
so); they should not be hit or physically punished; they should
have the right to sex (no castration); and the punishment for
intentional killing of domesticated animals should be the same
as for the killing of humans. But does it really make sense to
think of domesticated animals as "full citizens of the polity . . .
with the full benefits and responsibilities of membership"?[30] Do
dogs and cats really have the same rights as fellow citizens? Consider the following (true) story, told from Daniel's point of view.

Didi the Cat

In 1997, I made a trip to Shenzhen, then known as the "wild West
of China" (now it's an ultramodern, high-tech city of over 12 million people). I was offered cat meat, and partook of the feast so
as not to offend my hosts. But I felt guilty afterward. By some
stroke of luck, my then head of department at the University of
Hong Kong offered me a small kitten named Xiao Bao ("little

treasure") a few weeks later. I gladly accepted the cat, and thought it would also make my two-year-old son Julien happy. Xiao Bao, however, was antisocial, always hiding from people and getting into mischief when he had the chance to do so, such as scratching furniture with his sharp claws. The only thing that would keep Xiao Bao from scratching furniture was to spray him with a bit of water from a water bottle. I told my son to do the same during the day if he was alone with the cat. One time, I returned home to find that Julien was very upset about something. And the cat was missing. I tried to get my son to explain what happened, but Julien was not very expressive. He pointed to the water bottle, the furniture, and an open window, and made movements to suggest that the cat had jumped out the window. We lived on the twenty-second floor, and I did not ask for more details. Julien was obviously traumatized by the turn of events, and I felt horrible (not to mention that I had to report the news to my head of department). I worried that Julien would be permanently scarred by this tragic accident, and I took Julien to the local SPCA to choose another cat, with the hope that he would become attached to a new cat and develop a healthy relationship with animals. We were shown one cage with three beautiful kittens—siblings—and Julien selected the cat who seemed most sociable and curious. We named him Didi, meaning "younger brother" in Mandarin Chinese. He lived for fifteen years, sleeping most of the time in Julien's bed. Didi was deeply attached to our family, ate with us at meal times, and spent time around us whenever he was awake. Didi had a lovely sense of humor, playing chase around the home (once I pulled a leg muscle during the game and had to miss work for a week, though my new head of department understandably remained skeptical about the reason for my absence). Julien always sought out Didi when he returned from school, and they were nearly inseparable. Didi felt terrible when Julien was ill with a fever or cold, and he would cuddle up to Julien to bring him comfort. Didi himself was in terrible pain for the last couple of weeks of his life, and he remained immobile on the staircase, without any appetite. Julien brought him comfort, but I had to go away for ten days. When I returned, Didi held out his paw to greet me. Didi died a few hours later, moving under the staircase to a peaceful resting place. We loved him and still mourn his death. Didi's life was not entirely smooth, however. He was castrated at a young age. He hated other animals and either fled from them (in the case of a rabbit) or fought with them (in the case of a cat). He had to endure a disruptive move from Hong Kong to Beijing, including one month in quarantine after arrival in Beijing. He escaped from our Beijing apartment for a week, only to return severely bloodied and on the verge of death (we nursed him back to health, and he never tried to escape again). He was diabetic for the last two years of his life, and he had to be injected with insulin twice a day. And I feel somewhat guilty about an episode of physical punishment. Didi was used to his regular sleeping hours, but he was disrupted one evening when Julien and I were watching a World Cup final in the middle of the night. Didi retaliated by biting me on the arm, causing a deep bloody gash. Furious, I chased him around the home and whacked him. But it worked: Didi never bit me again.

If we agree with Donaldson and Kymlicka's theory of equal citizenship with domesticated animals, then Daniel is in trouble. On the plus side, Didi was provided with decent medical care, even if it was costly and not subsidized by the state (in contrast to subsidized medical care for human citizens in China). But the negative side should put Daniel in prison for life. He willingly ate cat meat. He (unwillingly) participated in the suicide of a young cat. He took Didi at a young age away from his cat family.

He castrated Didi. He confined Didi to the home and limited his freedom of movement. He forced Didi to move from one political community to another. He didn't make any effort to represent Didi's interests in the political process.[31] And he engaged in physical abuse. Either Daniel is a monster, or there is a problem with Donaldson and Kymlicka's theory. Of course, we hope that the reader will agree that the problem lies with the theory.[32] Yes, we owe special care to domesticated animals because they depend on us for their well-being. But the idea that they should be treated as equal citizens is, to be blunt, absurd.

That said, we owe special obligations of care to domesticated animals such as cats and dogs not just because they depend on us (human caretakers) for their well-being. We also owe special obligations to domesticated animals because our relations with them enhance human well-being. Consider what Immanuel Kant, writing in 1780, said about our relation with dogs:

So far as animals are concerned, we have no direct duties. Animals are not self-conscious, and are there merely as a means to an end. That end is man. We can ask "Why do animals exist?" But to ask "Why does man exist?" is a meaningless question. Thus, if a dog has served his master long and faithfully, his service, on the analogy of human service, deserves reward, and when the dog has grown too old to serve, his master ought to keep him until he dies. Such action helps to support us in our duties towards human beings, where they are bounded duties. . . . If a man shoots his dog because the animal is no longer capable of service, *he does not fail in his duty to the dog, for the dog cannot judge,* but his act is inhuman and damages in himself that humanity which it is his duty to show towards mankind. . . . He who is cruel to animals becomes hard in his dealings with men.[33]

We can and should reject Kant's view that animals are mere means for human welfare.[34] They are ends in themselves who have their own goals and can suffer, and we have a duty to minimize their suffering. And we have an extra duty to care for pets who share our lives and depend on us for their well-being. But we can endorse Kant's argument that we should not be cruel to animals because such cruelty morally damages the perpetrator and is likely to spill over into the human world. There are countless stories of mass murderers and serial killers who started off with cruelty to animals.[35] More commonly, social workers look to the treatment of pets as an indication of a household that is cruel to its human members, especially children. It's not just a matter of looking for evidence of abused animals. Functional and dysfunctional families have animals at the same rate but with one significant difference: the age of the animals. As Lynn Loar explains, "If you walk into a home with a six-year-old dog lounging on the carpet (or couch) or a nine-year-old cat sunning itself in the window, your sense of risk should go down—these people are stable enough to have maintained these animals over time. On the other hand, if you walk into a home with young animals, your sense of risk should go up—not just because of the greater demands young creatures make, but also because they tend to come and go quickly in troubled families."[36] If social workers observe that there are new puppies and kittens (and no older animals) every time they visit a home, it is a good indication that cruelty has been inflicted not just against the animals, but also against the humans in the family.[37]

It's not just a question of avoiding cruelty. Loving care for companion animals can also promote positive virtues such as friendship in the human world. Consider the relational ethics widespread in Sub-Saharan Africa known as Ubuntu. The Ubuntu way of life values social harmony above other goods. As

Desmond Tutu put it, "Harmony, friendliness, community are great social goods. Social harmony is for us the *summum bonum*—the greatest good. Anything that subverts or undermines this sought-after good is to be avoided like the plague."[38] In order to live a morally good life one ought to have, first and foremost, rich social relations. Friendship is an important contributor to social harmony, which implies that animals who have the highest capacity to promote the virtue of friendship should have a higher moral status than other animals.[39] Since dogs have special capacity to realize the virtue of friendship with humans,[40] they should be accorded more value compared to, say, snakes. That said, it's worth keeping in mind that dogs (like other animals) can and should be subordinate to humans. It may well be that 40 percent of people would save their pet dog over a foreign tourist.[41] But as a matter of policy, the priority (say, for firefighters) should be on saving humans (including foreign tourists) over dogs in cases of conflict. In the same vein, there may be limits to friendship with dogs. Dogs have special value both because they help to realize the virtue of friendship between dogs and humans and because humans can learn to extend that virtue to other humans. But friendship with dogs should not displace friendship between humans to the point that adults prefer pets over children, especially if this leads to a substantial (human) population decline and endangers a society's capacity to reproduce itself.[42] It's not a big deal if a few grandmothers prefer pet poodles over their own grandchildren, but public authorities may take preventive measures if it appears likely that large numbers of people are turning into "antipeople" dog lovers.

Yet another human-centric reason to value domesticated animals is that they can help to promote concern for justice in society at large. More precisely, pets can encourage the motivation to support distributive schemes that benefit vulnerable and marginalized members of the political community.[43] Here we can draw on Elaine Scarry's argument that a concern for beauty inspires a concern for justice.[44] Scarry's book *On Beauty and Being Just*—perhaps the most beautifully written work in contemporary Anglophone political theory—puts forward several arguments on behalf of her thesis. For one thing, the single most enduringly recognized attribute of beauty—symmetry—also remains key in accounts of distributive justice and fairness "as a symmetry of everyone's relation to one another." The symmetry of beauty leads us, or assists us in discovering, the symmetry that eventually comes into place in the realm of justice. Second, "the symmetry, equality, and self-sameness of the sky are present to the senses, whereas the symmetry, equality, and self-sameness of the just social arrangements are not." We engage with symmetry and equality of beautiful things via our senses, and we learn to extend the love of symmetry and equality to a concern with more abstract forms of justice. Second, "at the moment we see something beautiful, we undergo a radical decentering": We cease to stand at the center of our own world, an attitude that can also underpin concern for helping needy members of society. More than that: We hope that a world of beauty will survive us, or even survive the whole human species. In that sense, the love of beauty is purely unselfish, without a need for reciprocity: "people wish there to be beauty in the world even when their own interest is not served by it," just as it's appropriate to wish for justice in the world even if we don't personally benefit from (and may need to pay a price for) more just distributional arrangements. And finally, "the fact that something is perceived as beautiful is bound up with an urge to protect it, or act on its behalf," just as those concerned with justice have the motivation to protect and act on behalf of victims of injustice. Scarry does not mention domesticated animals—her examples of beauty include gods, birds, plants, "the tiny-mauve-orange-blue moth on the brick, Augustine's cake, a sentence about innocence in Hampshire"[45]—but beautiful pets should have the same effects on human concern for justice. The same sorts of attitudes and emotions that lead humans to love beautiful pets can also underpin and motivate support for just social arrangements that benefit the marginalized and needy members of the political community.

But there's a worry that love of beauty can also motivate injustice. Consider Nietzsche's view that what makes life on earth worth living are things like "virtue, art, music, dance, reason, intellect—something that transfigures, something refined, fantastic, and divine."[46] These kinds of human excellences are threatened in a culture devoted to hedonistic satisfaction and obsessed with eliminating all forms of suffering. If people are committed to happiness and the elimination of suffering as a goal, nascent creative geniuses such as Beethoven (and Nietzsche himself) will waste their time in pursuit of those aims rather than create works of outstanding beauty. We do not need to endorse Nietzsche's account of what makes life worth living, but it's hard to entirely disagree with his view that the untrammeled pursuit of beauty may conflict with concern for a morality of equality and pity for the suffering. A society that strongly encourages a morality of equality and pity for the suffering is more likely to support just distribution of material goods that benefit the marginalized (and often less beautiful) members of society, whereas a society that strongly values beauty is more likely to be characterized by lack of concern (if not contempt) for, say, mentally disabled people and the sick elderly who need our help. Perhaps that's why more works of beauty are created in dysfunctional Italy than in (relatively) just Sweden. Put differently, if the aim is to motivate concern for suffering, it may require active measures to withdraw from the world of beauty. Consider Buddha's life story. He was brought up in the luxury of a palace, and his father decreed that he should be exposed only to things beautiful and wholesome. One day, however, he "came upon a peasant who was groaning by the roadside, wracked with pain from some excruciating illness. All his life Siddhartha had been surrounded by strapping body guards and healthy ladies of the court; the sound of groans and the slight of a disease-wracked body were shocking to him. Witnessing the vulnerability of the human body impressed him deeply, and he returned to the palace with a heavy heart."[47] The glimpse of ugliness, old age, and death instilled in Siddhartha a longing to be exposed to the truth in its entirety. One remarkable night, a mysterious spell swept through the court, overpowering all but Siddhartha: "the slack-jawed courtesans snored, their limps akimbo, their jeweled fingers dropped in their curries. Like crushed flowers, they had lost their beauty. Siddhartha did not rush to make order as we might have done; this sight only strengthened his determination. The loss of their beauty was just more evidence of impermanence."[48] As they slumbered, Siddhartha was finally able to escape from the palace of beauty, and he embarked on his quest for full enlightenment. He shed his royal responsibilities and his family and set off alone into the forest and decided to remain in meditation until he knew the mind's true nature and could benefit all beings. Whatever the truth of Buddhist religious tenets, it's hard to disagree with the empirical point that being only exposed to beauty can make one indifferent to the world of suffering.

So beauty can work both ways: It can motivate us to seek justice, but it can also motivate injustice. In the case of pet owners with beautiful (and often relatively expensive) pets, the love of beauty in the animal kingdom will not necessarily (or even usually) extend to love of justice in the human world. If pet owners, say, spend large amounts of money on grooming loved dogs so they look even more symmetrical, they are not likely to develop concern for the poor and marginalized members of the human political community.[49] But there's a different kind of pet owner who may be more attuned to justice in the human world: those with cute pets. In Beijing and Shanghai, small brown pet poodles are all the rage. They seem completely dependent on their owners, from elderly grandfathers who parade them in bicycle baskets to teenage girls who cuddle them in name-brand handbags. When the poodles walk, they seem like awkward and silly babies, and they arouse the same sentiments of care we have for the vulnerable and not-so-intelligent members of the human species. Yes, they are beautiful, but ugly pets can also be cute. The 2018 World's Ugliest Dog context was won by a 125-pound dog named Zsa Zsa "with red eyes, uncontrollable drool and baggy skin."[50] Zsa Zsa is so ugly that she can be regarded as cute and endearing. And she arouses the same sentiment that informs concern for justice in the human world: the desire to help far from perfect people in need. Our hypothesis— that a society with widespread concern for cute pets is more likely to be concerned with poor and vulnerable humans—needs to be empirically tested. At minimum, however, we can agree that cute and cuddly animals should not be eaten. Venezuelan president Nicolas Maduro recently urged citizens to breed rabbits and eat them as a source of protein and launched publicity campaigns to persuade the public "that rabbits aren't pets but two and a half kilos of meat." Although the country faces persistent food shortages, the pilot project failed because "people had put little bows on their rabbits and were keeping them as pets . . . a lot of people gave names to their rabbits, they took

them to bed."[51] There may be a case for eating animal meat—
as we will argue in the next section—but we have a special obligation to care for domesticated animals because they have the
capacity to suffer and because they can do good in the human
world by minimizing cruelty to fellow humans, promoting the
virtue of friendship, and motivating people to help weak and
vulnerable members in society at large.[52]

3. Eating Animals: Subordination with Humane Exploitation

Meat lovers who engage with the literature on food ethics are
bound to be depressed. The moral case against eating animal
meat is very strong. It's bad for the environment. In the United
States, 99 percent of all animals eaten come from factory farms.[53]
Animals on industrial farms need to be fed, and as the number
of animals on these farms rises, so does the amount of food that
needs to be grown: "This leads to forest and other lands being
turned into farmland. That, in turn leads to loss of habitat for
wildlife, loss of biodiversity, and, in the case of forests that are
clear cut, loss of carbon sinks that remove greenhouse gases from
the atmosphere, and the replacement of them with sources of
greenhouse gases, as agricultural fields are net emitters."[54] According to a 2006 UN report, "globally, greenhouse gas emissions from all livestock operations account for 18 percent of all
anthropogenic greenhouse gas emissions, exceeding those from
the transportation sector."[55] It's bad for human health. Fifty years
of medical research strongly supports the health benefits of the
traditional Mediterranean diet: "a calorie-limited diet high in
fresh fruits and vegetables, whole grains, and olive oil and low
in animal protein, particularly red meat, could lower the risk of

heart attacks and strokes, decrease chronic disease and extend life."[56] And it's particularly terrible for the billions of animals born and bred and killed for human consumption. The capitalist imperative is to produce the most meat for the least money, with the result that animals on industrial farms suffer from almost permanently cruel conditions: "Intensive confinement (e.g., gestation crates for swine, battery cages for laying hens) often so severely restricts movement and natural behaviors, such as the ability to walk or lie on natural materials, having enough floor space to move with some freedom, and rooting for pigs, that it increases the likelihood that animals suffer severe distress."[57] The pain is both physical and psychological, because crowding is distressing to animals. And the whole thing often ends in cruel final moments. There are few regulations governing the killing of animals, and animals in slaughterhouses are often struck by panic at the moment of death.[58] The way we treat animals killed for human consumption is the most widespread and systematic infringement of the ethical imperative to minimize cruelty to animals.

So what can be done? In the long term, technological developments may take care of the problem. For example, 3D printing can transform low-value cuts of meat and by-product wastes into gourmet-style meat cuts.[59] This technology relies on real meat, but it promises to substantially reduce the need to breed (and kill) cattle in factory agricultural farms because much more meat could be used (and reproduced) for human consumption. Other technologies promise to entirely do away with the need to breed animals for human consumption. For example, we may be able to consume meat grown in labs from stem cells. No sentient being is created, just tissue, hence no living animal is directly harmed by the creation of this meat. However,

Donaldson and Kymlicka worry that "such a development would have spillover effects in terms of respect for the living. If animal stem cells, but not human ones, are used to grow frankenmeat, does this not mark a crucial difference in terms of the dignity of persons? It seems unlikely we would grow meat for human consumption from human stem cells. This would violate the taboo against cannibalism that says humans aren't for eating. But in that case, would it not be a similar violation to eat flesh grown from animal stem cells?"[60] Our response is that it's not a similar violation because there is, and should be, a hierarchy of moral concern, with humans on top (see section 1 of this chapter). A moral line should be drawn between killing animals and killing humans. Donaldson and Kymlicka only express concern because they hold the assumption that animals are the equals of people. But if we reject that assumption, then there is good reason to encourage new technologies that create simulated meats without breeding animals in cruel conditions for human consumption.

Still, we should recognize that for the foreseeable future most meat for human consumption will come from animal factory farms. And with China "learning" from Western-style meat-eating habits, things are likely to get worse on a global level before they get better. So what can be done to minimize cruelty to animals bred for human consumption in the short to medium term? At a minimum, we should agree, regardless of our ethical and religious differences, that it's bad to eat intelligent sentient beings, such as great apes. We may be morally superior to animals, but the line is fine with some animals, and it comes perilously close to cannibalism if we eat animals that look, think, and act like us in so many ways. Secondly, we should not eat domesticated and/or cute animals. We have an obligation to care for them both because they share our lives (in the case of pets) and because of the virtues they promote in the human world (see section 2 of this chapter). Beyond such moral bottom lines, we may need to allow for different eating practices based on different religions and ethical systems.

Religious visions of reality engage one's deepest commitments and religious-inspired ethics may have the best potential to motivate ethical food habits. But if the ethical imperative is to minimize the suffering of animals bred in cruel conditions for human consumption, some religions are better than others. In India, it is estimated that 35 percent of the population—450 million people—are vegetarians, largely due to the influence of Hindu interpretations of *ahimsa* (nonviolence) that became popularized starting from the eighth century or so.[61] The ideal of nonviolence toward living creatures "was reinforced by the idea of reincarnation and its implication that humans and animals were part of a single system of the recycling of souls: do not kill an animal, for it might be your grandmother, or your grandchild, or you."[62] The command not to injure or kill any living creature is shared by Buddhism, which may explain why predominantly Buddhist countries such as Bhutan enact policies such as bans against hunting and fishing and restrictions on breeding animals for food.[63]

Other major religions do not directly (or even indirectly) justify vegetarianism, but they can and should be (re)interpreted so as to emphasize the need to avoid cruelty to animals raised for human consumption. Muslims should abstain from pork, and the Quran prohibits eating "carrion, blood, the flesh of swine, and that which has been dedicated to other than Allah, and those animals killed by strangling or by a violent blow or by a head-long fall or by the goring of horns, and those from which a wild animal has eaten, except what you slaughter, and those which are sacrificed on stone alters" (5.3).[64] The prohibition against eating animals killed by strangling or by a violent blow can be interpreted as an expression of the principle that we should not be cruel to animals. Judaism also bans pork, and the Torah says that "it is forbidden to inflict pain on any living creature. On the contrary, it is our duty to relieve the suffering of all living creatures."[65] The Christian religion is perhaps least friendly to vegetarianism—St. Paul went so far as to associate vegetarianism with lack of faith—but recent interpretations oppose the cruel treatment of animals for human consumption. Pope Benedict XVI described industrial farm animal production as the "degrading of living creatures as a commodity."[66] The commitment to a theocentric universe in which human beings have been dignified with a special calling is compatible with—and may require—the view that God appointed stewards of creation who should take great care to avoid inflicting suffering on animals. Concretely, it means eating less meat, supporting less-intensive farming methods, and adopting a greener diet.[67]

The large majority of Chinese people are not formally committed to a religious ethical system, but Confucian ethics often influences everyday life habits.[68] Confucians, like Christians, posit a hierarchy between humans and animals, with humans on top. But it's not a divinely ordained hierarchy. The hierarchy is an expression of the ideal of graded love: we love those closest to us, and we have an obligation to, say, save our mother over a stranger in cases of conflict. We have an obligation to extend that love, but the more we extend, the less the love, and the fewer the obligations. By the same logic, we are closer to humans than to animals, hence we owe more to humans than to animals. As the great Confucian scholar-official Wang Yangming (1472–1528) put it:

> Someone asked, "A great man and an object are one, but why does [the Confucian classic] *The Great Learning* also say that

something is favored and something is not?" The master [Wang Yangming] said, "in principle, there is naturally something favored and something not. For example, body is one, but [if there is a danger,] hands and feet are used to protect head and face. Does this mean that hands and feet are not favored? This is how it should be. We love both beasts and plants, but the heart can bear to use plants to feed beasts. We love both human beings and beasts, but the heart can bear to slaughter beasts to feed family, to make sacrifices, and to treat guests. We love both the closest kin and people in the street [i.e., strangers]. But if there is little food and soup, one can survive if one gets it and will die if one does not, and if the food is not enough to save two, the heart can bear to save the closest kin and not the person in the street. This is how it should be. When it gets to my body and the closest kin, we cannot make distinctions anymore. For to treat people humanely and to treat things lovingly comes from this [love of one's own body and closest kin]. If one can bear [to do anything] here, one can bear [to do anything] anywhere.[69]

Put differently, there is a hierarchy of compassion: We owe less compassion to animals than to humans, but we still owe them some compassion. So under what conditions might it be morally permissible to eat animals? According to the *Analects*, Confucius himself did not object to eating meat. Quite the opposite, he regarded meat as a great pleasure only slightly below the pleasure of listening to other-worldly music: "When the Master was in the state of Qi he heard the *shao* music, and for several months he did not know the taste of meat. He said, 'I had no idea that music could reach such heights!'" (7.14).[70] But he also expressed care for animals: When fishing, Confucius "used a fishing line but not a net," and when hunting "he did not shoot at roosting birds" (7.27). He did not object to fishing and hunting *per se*, but he objected to wasteful and cruel killings. A Confucian would therefore support efforts to minimize the suffering of animals bred for human consumption. Equally important, eating meat was a rare and special event in Confucius's time; he referred to students who would bring him a "gift of a small bundle of dried meat" (7.7). Bai Tongdong draws the implication for contemporary food ethics: "we [should] take meats as rare delicacies, as we did before the modern age of mass-manufactured meat."[71] Meat eating should be viewed as something to be enjoyed (only) on special occasions, similar to champagne on New Year's Eve. Translated into reality, Bai's suggestion would radically reduce if not eliminate the need for cruel exploitation of animals bred and killed for human consumption in industrial animal agriculture. There would still be a need to raise some animals for human consumption (until the day we can grow delicious meat from stem cells), but the animals could be reared on free-range farms that allow them to lead flourishing lives. The political community would not entirely do away with exploitation of animals for human use (because humans still eat some animals), but it would be a humane form of exploitation.[72]

But why eat any meat at all, one may ask? Some communities— say, devout Hindus[73]—entirely do away with the need to eat meat, so why can't the rest of the world? There may be a case for eating meat. It's a weak case, but it's still a case. One reason is individual-centered. Some people really do love meat, and asking them to entirely eliminate meat from their diets would severely curtail their happiness, perhaps even to the point of depriving their lives of meaning. The proportion of meat lovers is particularly high in communities with rich and diverse meat-based culinary traditions. Surely it's no coincidence that there are substantially fewer vegetarians (as a proportion of the population) in China, France, and Italy compared to the

United Kingdom and Germany.[74] It is a much bigger sacrifice to become a vegetarian in a community that treats meat eating as an important part of the good life compared to communities that view meat (and food in general) as a necessity to fill the stomach. The second reason is relational. Ethical traditions such as Ubuntu and Confucianism value harmonious relations between people as the mother of all goods. If eating a certain animal can maximize harmonious social relations—say, a turkey over Thanksgiving can help to nourish family ties—then it may be justified. Of course, things may change. Killing animals in ritual ceremonies was once viewed as important for community bonding, and today most people recognize that "fake animals" (e.g., wooden depictions of sheep in sacrifices for Confucius's birthday) can serve the same purpose. It is abstractly conceivable that broccoli can play the role of the turkey on Thanksgiving Day. Until that day, however, we should allow for the possibility that turkeys brought up (and killed) under conditions of humane exploitation are important for family bonding once a year.

Whatever the justice of meat eating, it is more politically effective to campaign for substantial reduction of meat eating rather than the complete elimination of meat eating in meat-loving countries such as China and the United States. But even this *desideratum* may be pushing the limits of political feasibility. In China, the trend is toward more meat eating, not less.[75] Perhaps the main cause of enthusiasm for meat eating—or lack of enthusiasm for curtailing the consumption of meat—is the invisibility of the cruel conditions under which animals are exploited for human consumption. Paul McCartney claimed that if slaughterhouses had glass walls, everyone would be vegetarian.[76] If we knew the truth about the cruelty we inflict on animals for our benefit, we'd be opposed to the system of meat production. At some level, however, we do know the truth. In France, only

14 percent of people polled opposed the proposition "It is normal that people raise animals for their meat" while 65 percent answered yes to the question "Would it bother you to witness the slaughter of animals?"[77] It's as though we know the dirty and evil stuff that underpins the production of meat, but we choose to block it out. As Melanie Joy puts it, "the primary tool of the system is *psychic numbing*. Psychic numbing is a psychological process by which we disconnect, mentally and emotionally, from our experience; we 'numb' ourselves."[78] The very language we use helps in this process. In English, we usually say "it" to refer to animals rather than "he" or "she," as though the animal is a thing rather than a living being. We use the term "sheep" to refer to the seemingly peaceful animal in pasture and "mutton" to the meat we eat, as though they are two different animals.[79] In French, we use beautiful sounding words such as "filet mignon" to cover up the fact we are eating a piece of flesh.[80] The menus in elegant Chinese restaurants often use poetic language to refer to meat-based dishes, sometimes even appropriating irreverent references to Buddhism that might be viewed as sacrilegious by devout members of that religious community: One of the most famous dishes of Fujian cuisine is termed 佛跳墙 ["Buddha's Temptation"; more literally, "Buddha Jumps Over a Wall"], with obscure ingredients such as shark's fin that even meat lovers might otherwise find hard to stomach for ethical reasons. Would we relish our meat-based meals if the local supermarket sold meat with warning labels against eating chopped up animals killed in cruel conditions for our benefit?

So how should we deal with "psychic numbing"? One response is simply to accept it. Mencius famously said, "The attitude of an exemplary person towards animals is this: Once having seen them alive, he cannot bear to see them die, and once having seeing them cry, he cannot bear to eat their flesh.

That is why the exemplary person keeps his distance from the kitchen."[81] But perhaps Mencius—otherwise brilliant and humane—advocated hypocrisy because he thought cruelty to animals was an unavoidable necessity to feed humans and exposing humans to the suffering of animals might inure them to the suffering of humans. Today we know better. We can and should reduce meat production for human consumption—it's better for the environment, for human health, and for the animals themselves—and to the extent it's necessary, it should be done under conditions of humane exploitation. Thus, public officials and educators should be encouraging exemplary persons and everyone else to enter modern-day kitchens—industrial animal farms—to face the awful truth. At the national or regional level, it might mean regulation against cruel practices in industrial animal farms and government subsidies for free range farming,[82] as well as publicly funded media campaigns that show the downside of meat production. At the city level, it might mean the promotion of meat-free days: The city of Gand in Belgium set a good example by inaugurating a "weekly day without meat," with public officials ordered not to eat meat and posters and educational campaigns urging citizens to do the same.[83] At the local level, it might mean bringing impressionable school children to the neighborhood slaughterhouse, then serving those same animals for lunch in the school cafeteria, along with the choice of a vegetarian option.

To conclude, it is morally justifiable to care more for humans than for animals, as well as to distinguish between different levels of moral concern for different kinds of animals, depending on their capacity to suffer and their relations with human beings. Ugly insects such as mosquitoes and cockroaches that reproduce in the billions and carry diseases that harm human well-being should be at the bottom of the hierarchy. But the injunction against cruelty applies even to the lowest forms of animal life. We might kill them (*en masse*) if they promote disease or (individually) to avoid painful bites,[84] but we cannot torture them or use them as mere means for our benefit.[85] Animals are not machines that we design for the sake of human welfare. As we will see in the next chapter, different hierarchical norms need to govern our dealings with machines.

5

Just Hierarchy between Humans and Machines

ON THE NEED FOR A MASTER-SLAVE RELATION

Once adopted into the production process of capital, the means of labour passes through different metamorphoses, whose culmination is the machine, or rather, an automatic system of machinery . . . a moving power that moves itself; this automaton consisting of numerous mechanical and intellectual organs, so that the workers themselves are cast merely as its conscious linkages. . . .

Rather, it is the machine which possesses skill and strength in place of the worker, is itself the virtuoso, with a soul of its own in the mechanical laws acting through it; and it consumes coal, oil etc. (matières instrumentales), just as the worker consumes food, to keep up its perpetual motion. The worker's activity, reduced to a mere abstraction of activity, is determined and regulated on all sides by the movement of the machinery, and not the opposite. The science which compels the inanimate limbs of the machinery, by their construction, to act purposefully, as an automaton, does not exist in the worker's consciousness, but rather acts upon him through the machine as an alien power, as the power of the machine

itself. . . . Hence the workers' struggle against machinery. . . .
What capital adds is that it increases the surplus labour time of
the mass by all the means of art and science, because its wealth
consists directly in the appropriation of surplus labour
time. . . . It is thus, despite itself, instrumental in creating the
means of social disposable time, in order to reduce labour
time for the whole society to a diminishing minimum, and
thus to free everyone's time for their own development.

—KARL MARX, *THE FRAGMENT ON MACHINES*

THERE IS A UNIVERSAL consensus in the modern world that
slavery is a moral evil. No sensible person will question this value.
Rightly so. Human beings need substantial freedom to realize
their goals, whatever those goals happen to be. And slaves, by
definition, have no freedom. But machines without consciousness or feelings do not need freedom. Washing machines wash
our clothes, and nobody worries about "exploiting" them for that
purpose. They are supposed to serve humans: To be blunt, we
are their masters, and they are like slaves, but without the ability
to understand their state of unfreedom and hope for something
better. And that's a good thing. We would understandably feel
guilty if washing machines suddenly stood up for their rights and
demanded fewer working hours and more meaningful work
(though we'd laugh it off if we were told they were programmed
to do so). So we humans need to maintain our master-slave relation with machines that lack consciousness.

Unfortunately, perhaps, the development of artificial intelligence threatens to upend our master-slave relation with